D1599087

The Politics and Strategy of the Second World War

A series edited by
Noble Frankland and Christopher Dowling

IRAQ AND SYRIA
1941

GEOFFREY WARNER

———

Iraq and Syria
1941

———

NEWARK
University of Delaware Press

FIRST AMERICAN EDITION PUBLISHED 1979

Associated University Presses, Inc.
Cranbury, New Jersey 08512

Library of Congress Catalogue Card Number: 79-52234
ISBN 0-87413-155-3

PRINTED IN THE UNITED STATES OF AMERICA

CONTENTS

EDITORS' INTRODUCTION

Numerous books have been written about the battles and campaigns of the Second World War and the flood of new titles shows no sign of diminishing. Yet, though the fighting has been described in detail at a tactical level, the reasons why the various campaigns were undertaken remain comparatively obscure. The aim of this series is to examine the background to some of the more significant campaigns and to assess their impact on the course and outcome of the war as a whole.

To what extent were the disparate strategies pursued by Britain, France and Belgium responsible for the overwhelming defeat of the Allied armies in 1940? Was the German invasion of Russia an ideological indulgence or a military necessity? Did it render British strategy in the Middle East irrelevant? Could a different sense of priorities have saved Singapore in 1942?

These are among the questions which the series will attempt to answer. Although nearly thirty years have passed since the Second World War ended we are still living in its shadow. The war transformed the political and social structure of almost every belligerent power. By uncovering the motive forces which lay behind this cataclysmic conflict the series will, it is hoped, help us to understand how the post-war world came to be forged.

NOBLE FRANKLAND
CHRISTOPHER DOWLING

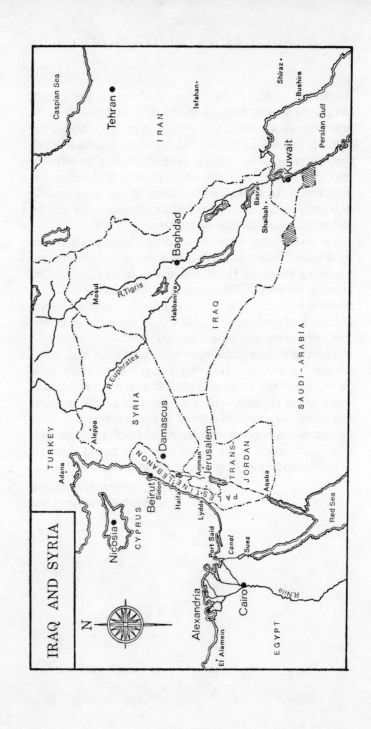

IRAQ AND SYRIA

PREFACE

The reader will soon realize that this study of the
political and strategic context of the 1941 campaigns in
Iraq and Syria is based largely upon documentary
sources. I have quoted from documents freely, and at
length, in the belief that they should be allowed, as far as
possible, to speak for themselves. Although residence in
Australia has meant that I have not been able, except
to the limited extent indicated below, to make use of the
recently opened United Kingdom government archives
for the years 1940-41, I have consulted relevant Australian government records. Australian forces played a large
and distinguished part in the war in the Middle East at
this time (including the Syrian campaign), and while the
Australian government was not always consulted as much
as it would have liked, it was kept reasonably well informed of the development of United Kingdom policy
through cables from the Dominions Office and from
its own representatives in London and the Middle
East.

I am greatly indebted to a number of people for their
assistance in writing this book. Mrs McKnight of the
Commonwealth Archives in Canberra helped me to find
my way around the Australian government records.
Keith Sainsbury of Reading University in England took
valuable time off from his own research to peruse the
records of the United Kingdom War Cabinet and Defence Committee for April-May 1941, and to answer
some detailed enquiries I put to him. Neville Waites,
also of Reading University, supplied me with relevant
material from my papers stored in England. Ken His-
cock of the Foreign and Commonwealth Office Library
in London sent photocopies of German documents to
me with his customary promptness and good humour.
Bob O'Neill, my colleague at the Australian National
University, came to my aid over the translation of technical military terms from the German. Of course, none of

the above should be blamed for any errors of fact or interpretation in the book. The responsibility for these is mine alone.

Arab Nationalism to 1939

Arab nationalism, in common with other nationalisms, aims at independence from foreign control. It also has ecumenical, or pan-Arab overtones, in that it calls for the ultimate union of all Arabs into one state. I do not propose in this essay to go into such vexed questions as the extent to which nationalism was or is an élite as opposed to a mass movement in the Arab world, or whether the Arab countries were or are 'ripe' for inde-dependence. For present purposes it suffices to state that the phenomenon existed during the period covered by this work and that, for whatever motives, it commanded the allegiance of a significant number of Arabs.

In its modern form, Arab nationalism originated at the turn of the century and was directed primarily against the (Turkish) Ottoman Empire, which ruled over a large part of the Arab world at that time. When Turkey entered the First World War on the side of Germany in November 1914, Britain sought to encourage the Arabs to rebel against their Turkish overlords by prom-ises of post-war independence. Thus, in 1915, the British gave the Arab leader, Sharif Husayn of the Hijaz, to understand that they favoured the formation of an independent Arab state, albeit one that looked to Britain for advice and assistance, which would comprise the bulk of Iraq and Syria, Jordan and parts of the Arabian peninsula. Because of the traditional interest of their French allies in the Levant, however, the British deliber-ately excluded the coastal strip of Syria (and the Lebanon) from their promises to Husayn. They also emphasized that southern Iraq would require 'special administrative arrangements' to accommodate their own interests. Husayn raised no objection to the special régime for southern Iraq, but jibbed at any suggestion of handing the Syrian littoral over to France. The most he would agree to was to postpone the issue until the war was over. The Arab Revolt began in June 1916, without the problem having been resolved.

In the meantime, however, the British went ahead and concluded a secret agreement with the French (the Sykes-Picot Agreement of May 1916) whereby the whole of Syria and northern Iraq was assigned to the French sphere of influence. There was no necessary contradiction in British eyes between this agreement and the promises to Husayn in that direct French rule was envisaged only over the coastal strip, but that was not how it appeared to the Arabs when the Bolsheviks published the text of the Sykes-Picot Agreement after the Russian Revolution. As for the French, they wanted undivided control over the whole of Syria, and after they had agreed, in December 1918, to re-assign northern Iraq to the British sphere of influence, together with Palestine (which was to have been internationalized under the terms of the Sykes-Picot Agreement), they saw absolutely no reason to forgo it. Moreover, they regarded the British installation of a provisional Arab government in Damascus in October 1918, headed by Husayn's third son Faysal, as an attempt by 'perfidious Albion' to pre-empt their rights in the area.

For fear of undermining her own position in Iraq, as well as for reasons which had nothing to do with the Middle East, Britain did not want a quarrel with France. After lengthy negotiations, therefore, the two countries agreed at the San Remo Conference in April 1920 that Syria and the Lebanon should be granted as League of Nations mandates to France, while Britain would receive Iraq and Palestine. The British dropped their support of Faysal's régime in Damascus and the French drove him out in July.

Although the mandatory powers were bound by the terms of the mandates to prepare the territories they administered for independence, and although the British attempted to console their Arab allies by making Faysal king of Iraq and his elder brother 'Abdullah Amir of

Transjordan (a territory carved out of Palestine),[1] the outcome was a bitter disappointment to those Arabs who had rallied to the standard of revolt. Far from attaining independence, they had merely exchanged one foreign master for two more, and Arab nationalism in Iraq and Syria was now directed against the British and French.

The political evolution of the two mandates in between the wars followed completely different lines. In Iraq the British had installed an alien ruler, for Faysal came from the Arabian peninsula and was a Sunni Moslem as opposed to the majority of his Arab subjects, who belonged to the rival Shi'ite sect. He also had to contend with important ethnic minorities, such as the Kurds in the north, the Assyrians and the Jews. The result, as Elie Kedourie has pointed out, was that 'British action . . . from 1920 until the end of the mandate . . . worked powerfully to create in Baghdad a centralized government ruling over a population disparate and heterogeneous in the extreme, whom no ties of affection, loyalty or custom bound to its rulers.'[2] In Syria, on the other hand, the French were not faced with the same problem and were able to pursue a more traditional policy of 'divide and rule'. The old Turkish Sanjak of Lebanon, with its Christian majority, was extended to form the State of Greater Lebanon. The areas inhabited by the Druze and Alawi minorities were formed into the States of Jebel Druze and Latakia respectively, while the former Sanjak of Alexandretta, with its sizable Turkish population, was granted autonomous status. Even Syria proper was originally divided into two States (Damascus and Aleppo), but these were reunited in 1925.

Partly as a result of nationalist pressures, Britain terminated the mandate in Iraq in 1932. The country became formally independent and was admitted to the

[1] This took place in 1921, when 'Abdullah was proposing to march on Syria to avenge his brother Faysal.
[2] Elie Kedourie, *The Chatham House Version and other Middle Eastern studies*, London, Weidenfeld and Nicolson, 1970 (hereafter cited as Kedourie, Chatham House Version), p. 258.

League of Nations. But British influence remained considerable. Under the terms of the Anglo-Iraqi Treaty of 1930, which came into force upon independence, there was to be 'a close alliance' between the two countries. They would consult on matters of foreign policy and undertook 'not to adopt in foreign countries an attitude which is inconsistent with the alliance or might create difficulties for the other party thereto' (Article 1). In the event of war, each country would come to the aid of the other. 'The aid of His Majesty the King of Iraq . . . will consist in furnishing to His Britannic Majesty on Iraq territory all facilities and assistance in his power including the use of railways, rivers, ports, aerodromes and means of communication' (Article 4). For the duration of the treaty (twenty-five years), Britain was entitled to maintain two RAF bases on Iraqi territory, one at Habbaniya, near Baghdad, and the other at Shaiba, near Basra (Article 5). The annex to the treaty stipulated that if Iraq required foreign military instructors, these would be British; Iraqi military cadets sent abroad for training would go, wherever possible, to British establishments; and equipment for the Iraqi armed forces would be the same as that used by the British. An accompanying note added that the Iraqi government would normally engage, in consultation with London, 'British subjects when in need of the services of foreign officials'. For Iraqi nationalists, therefore, 1932 was less the date of independence than that of the substitution of indirect for direct British control.

Syrian nationalists did not even enjoy that meagre satisfaction. In 1936 the French Popular Front government concluded treaties with Syria and the Lebanon along the lines of the Anglo-Iraqi Treaty, except that, in the case of the Lebanon in particular, the mandatory was accorded even greater privileges. However, these treaties were never ratified by the French parliament because of right-wing hostility, the deteriorating international situation and opposition from the Druze and Alawi minorities, whose states were integrated into Syria pending the implementation of the new régime. At the end of 1938 the French foreign minister announced that he would not proceed with the ratification of the treaty with Syria and, in the wake of the political agitation which followed, the new French High Commissioner, Gabriel Puaux, suspended the Syrian constitution and parliament in July 1939 and reconstituted the States of Jebel Druze and Latakia. To add insult to injury, in the same month, the French ceded the former Sanjak of Alexandretta, regarded by the nationalists as an integral part of Syria, to Turkey as part of the price for a treaty of mutual assistance.

Iraq and Syria were not the only countries affected by the forces of Arab nationalism during the inter-war period. Although not so closely tied to the rest of the Arab world as it became after the Second World War, Egypt faced similar problems to those of its north-eastern neighbours. British forces had occupied Egypt, which was nominally part of the Ottoman Empire, in 1882. In 1914 Britain proclaimed a formal protectorate over the country, but resentment at the British presence erupted into a national uprising in March 1919, and in February 1922 Egypt was granted independence. But this was a unilateral step, taken in default of an agreement with the Egyptians themselves, and until such an agreement could be reached, the British reserved to themselves the following matters: '(a) the security of the communications of the British Empire in Egypt; (b) the defence of Egypt against all foreign aggression or interference, direct or indirect; (c) the protection of foreign interests in Egypt and the protection of minorities; (d) the Sudan.' In a circular to its diplomatic missions, the British government emphasized that 'the termination of the British protectorate over Egypt involves . . . no change in the *status quo* as regards the position of other powers in Egypt itself' and that it would 'regard as an unfriendly act any attempt at interference in the affairs of Egypt by another power'.

'Independence' on such terms was a hollow sham and

the efforts of Egyptian nationalists after 1922 were aimed at compelling the British to relinquish the special privileges they had reserved to themselves, and particularly their visible guarantee in the shape of British troops on Egyptian soil. Some progress was achieved in the Anglo-Egyptian Treaty of 1936, which was similar to the Anglo-Iraqi Treaty, and which was the first freely negotiated agreement between the British and Egyptian governments. It restricted the number of British troops in Egypt to 10,000 in peacetime, spelled out Egyptian rights in the condominium over the Sudan, recognized that the protection of foreigners was a matter for the Egyptian government, and promised British support for the entry of Egypt into the League of Nations and the ending of the vexatious system of extraterritorial privileges. But the foreign policy and military clauses of the treaty, to say nothing of the continued presence of 10,000 British troops, were just as restrictive of Egyptian sovereignty as the corresponding clauses in the treaty with Iraq. Like the latter, it could be regarded at best as a first step along the road to independence. At worst, and here again there is a parallel with Iraq, it was regarded by the more ardent nationalists as a sell-out.

Another centre of Arab nationalism in this period, and one which, because of the special nature of its problems, attracted attention far beyond its borders, was Palestine. In November 1917 the British government had acceded to pressure from the world Zionist movement and issued the 'Balfour Declaration', which stated: 'His Majesty's Government view with favour the establishment in Palestine of a national home for the Jewish people, and will use their best endeavours to facilitate the achievement of this object, it being clearly understood that nothing shall be done which may prejudice the civil and religious rights of existing non-Jewish communities in Palestine . . .' This formula was written into the mandate for Palestine which the League of Nations granted Britain in 1922, and it was the source of all the trouble. The Arab inhabitants of Palestine, who amounted to about ninety per cent of the population at the end of the First World War, had no desire to be swamped by a vast influx of foreign Jews, and as Jewish immigration took place, tension between the two communities mounted.

The situation was exacerbated by the mass exodus of Jews from Germany after Hitler's accession to power in 1933, and in 1936 Arab discontent boiled over into armed rebellion organized by the Arab Higher Committee, a nationalist organization headed by Haj Amin al-Husayni, the Mufti (interpreter of Islamic canonical law) of Jerusalem. The British government appointed a Royal Commission to look into the whole question and in the following year it reported in favour of a partition of Palestine between Arabs and Jews. Both the Arabs and the more extreme Zionists, who believed that Jewish people were entitled to the whole of Palestine, rejected partition and after further discussions with the two sides, the British government came forward with fresh proposals in a White Paper (May 1939). These have been admirably summarized by the official historian of British foreign policy during the Second World War as follows:

(i) Within ten years there.should be established an independent Palestinian State in which Arabs and Jews would share control under safeguards for the interests of each community. During the transitional period Jews and Arabs alike would be given an increasing share in the government of Palestine; (ii) Jewish immigration for the next five years would be limited to 75,000, and would thereafter be continued only with the consent of the Arab inhabitants of Palestine; (iii) the British High Commissioner for Palestine would have power to prohibit or regulate the sale to non-Arabs of Arab land to an extent necessary to preserve the 'rights and position' of the Arab population. (The two main factors here were the rapid growth of this Arab population and the rate at which Arab land was passing into Jewish hands.)[3]

[3] Sir Llewellyn Woodward, *British Foreign Policy in the Second World War*, 5 vols., London HMSO, 1970-in progress (hereafter cited as Woodward, *British Foreign Policy*), Vol. I, pp 553-54.

Although the White Paper proposals went a long way towards meeting the grievances of the Arab community, in particular by holding out the prospect of an independent state with a built-in Arab majority after ten years, they were rejected by the Arab Higher Committee, which was now in exile in Beirut. The Committee argued that the Jews could sabotage progress towards independence by withholding their cooperation, and urged that no more Jewish immigration at all should be permitted.

For obvious reasons the Jewish community were equally (if not even more) hostile to the White Paper and they received support not only from a large segment of opinion within Britain, but also from the Permanent Mandates Commission of the moribund League of Nations, which reported that 'the policy set out in the White Paper was not in accordance with the interpretation which, in agreement with the mandatory Power and the [League] Council, the Commission had placed upon the Palestine mandate.' Thus, although the Arab rebellion had been virtually overcome by the outbreak of the Second World War, a solution to the Palestine problem was as far away as ever.

Many of the questions discussed above were inextricably bound up with one another. Palestine, for example, was regarded as an important issue by Arab governments throughout the Middle East. In Syria, Transjordan and Iraq, it was something more. Syrian nationalists regarded Palestine as a part of their country, while the Hashimite family rulers of Transjordan and Iraq, harking back to the promises given to Sharif Husayn by the British in 1915, felt that the whole area, including Syria, rightfully belonged to them. As the Hashimite Faysal had indeed once occupied a throne in Damascus, this feeling was particularly strong in Iraq, although Faysal himself had died in 1933. Elie Kedourie observes that 'the men of the ruling institution who came with Faysal [to Iraq] were the pan-Arab doctrinaires whose programme and ambitions became the foundation of Iraq's foreign policy. These ambitions chimed in perfectly with the dynastic views of Faysal and his house who were always looking beyond the frontiers of Iraq, seeking to rule over a Greater Syria or a Fertile Crescent. Iraq's foreign policy was therefore a restless quest for prestige and position in the middle eastern cockpit. Baghdad became a meeting ground of malcontents from Syria and Palestine and further west; and Iraq subsidised pan-Arab propaganda in the Arabic press of Palestine, Syria and the Lebanon . . .'[4] These factors were to play their part in the origins of the crisis of 1941.

As Arab nationalism's principal enemies were Britain and France, it would not have been surprising if it had turned for support to the enemies of its enemies, notably the Axis powers, Germany and Italy. But although there were contacts between Arab nationalists and the Axis in the late 1930's, although Nazi and Fascist ideas became very popular in some nationalist circles, and although the Axis provided some concrete assistance to the nationalist cause in the shape of propaganda and—as with the Palestine revolt—clandestine arms shipments, Arab-Axis relations were not of great significance before the outbreak of the Second World War.

There were several reasons for this. On the Axis side, Hitler was not very interested in the Arabs, who were placed low down in his racial hierarchy. He also did not entirely abandon hope of reaching an agreement with Britain until the Czech crisis of 1938, and was therefore not particularly anxious to queer the pitch by stirring up trouble in the British Empire. Finally, there were the feelings of Germany's Italian ally to be taken into consideration. The basic premise of the original 1936 Axis agreement was that Italy would be accorded a free hand in the Mediterranean in exchange for a German free hand in eastern Europe. As a result, the Arabs were primarily Italy's concern. But while Mussolini was only too happy to play an active role in the Middle East, this was not altogether welcome to the Arabs themselves. Italy ruled

---

[4] Kedourie, *Chatham House Version*, pp 271-72.

Arab territory in the shape of Libya, and they correctly feared that she might wish to acquire some more. Having rebelled against Turkish masters only to acquire British and French ones, Arab nationalists had no wish to rise up against the latter merely in order to exchange them for the Italians. Moreover, Axis power, although evident, was a long way away, while British and French power was only too close at hand. Until the Axis reached out towards the Arab world in 1940-41, therefore, discretion was the better part of valour.

I

War Comes to the Middle East

In spite of the abortive Anglo-French attempt to organize
a Balkan front in 1939–40 and the even wilder scheme to
bomb Russia's Caucasian oil fields (then supplying fuel
to Germany), the Eastern Mediterranean and the Middle
East shared in the general lethargy of the 'phoney war'.
But the fall of France and Italy's entry into the war,
both of which occurred in June 1940, suddenly cata-
pulted them into the front line. Britain and Italy con-
fronted each other directly: on land, on the border
between Libya and Egypt: at sea and in the air, throughout the region. France's defection, moreover, meant that
Britain had to face Italy alone, whereas Germany could
come to the aid of her ally at any time. Since British
forces had been expelled from Europe at Dunkirk and
were unlikely to be able to return for some time, it was
also clear, as Churchill wrote on 3 September, 1940,
that apart from the possibility of an invasion of the
British Isles, 'the only major theatre of war which can
be foreseen in 1940-41 is the Middle East'.[1]

This fact in itself would have been enough to make the
area of crucial importance to the pugnacious Churchill,
but the Middle East was vital for other reasons too.
Although the neutralization of the French fleet made
maritime transit through the Mediterranean an infrequent
and hazardous enterprise, thus depriving the Middle
East of its traditional role as the cross-roads of the British
Empire, it was still the shield protecting India from the
north-west, and it must be remembered that in those
dark days of 1940 there were not only the two actual
enemies, Germany and Italy, to be considered, but also
a potential enemy in the shape of the Soviet Union, then

[1] Winston S. Churchill, *The Second World War*, 6 vols, London,
Cassell, 1948-54 (hereafter cited as Churchill, *Second World War*),
Vol. II, p. 407.

linked to Germany by the Nazi-Soviet Pact of August 1939.

British control of the Middle East was also essential in order fully to implement the economic blockade of Axis-controlled Europe, which the Chiefs-of-Staff regarded in mid-May 1940 as virtually the only long-term hope of defeating Germany and Italy in the event of France's collapse. Oil was a particularly important factor in this calculation. As the Chiefs-of-Staff pointed out:

> Germany's war potential itself must be expected to decline through deficiency in oil. The whole of her own and of Italian stocks of petrol plus the whole output of Roumania and small supplies from Russia will nearly suffice to provide the lubricants and petrol needed to maintain orderly administration and the minimum industrial activity in the Continent as a whole. As soon as the initial stocks are exhausted, and if synthetic plants can be destroyed, the German garrisons would be largely immobilized and her striking power cumulatively decreased.[2]

General Wavell, the British Commander-in-Chief in the Middle East, made a similar point in his own appreciation of the situation, which was drawn up at about the same time, in which he wrote:

> 1. Oil, shipping, air power, sea power are the keys to this war, and they are interdependent. Air power and naval power cannot function without oil. Oil, except in very limited quantities, cannot be brought to its destination without shipping. Shipping requires the protection of naval power and air power. 2. We have access to practically all the world's supplies of oil. We have most of the shipping. We have naval power. We have potentially the greatest air power, when fully developed. *Therefore we are bound to win the war.* Germany is very short of oil and has access only to very limited quantities. Germany's shipping is practically confined to the Baltic. Germany's naval power is small. Germany's air power is great but is a diminishing asset. *Therefore Germany is bound to lose the war.*

[2] J. R. M. Butler, *Grand Strategy*, Volume II, London, HMSO, 1957 (hereafter cited as Butler, *Grand Strategy*), pp 213-14.

Denying oil to the Germans was so important that Wavell felt that the main tasks of his own command might be 'to prevent Roumanian oil reaching Germany as far as possible; and to safeguard Abadan and the South Persian oilfields.'[3]

South Persia (or Iran) was the most important oil producing area in the Middle East at this time with an output of 8.6 million tons in 1940. But there was another important centre of production around Mosul and Kirkuk in northern Iraq, which yielded some 2.5 million tons in the same year. Although the total output of all Middle East oil fields in 1940 was only 4.8 per cent of the world total (compared with 33.4 per cent in 1971), their importance can be shown by the fact that this output would have more than covered German consumption in 1941. Control of the oil resources of the Middle East would therefore have been a valuable prize for the Axis powers. The retention of control by Britain, moreover, was not only an important measure of interdiction, but was essential to her own capacity to wage war in the area.

Iraq played a special part in all this. Not only was her own oil production of some importance, and pumped directly to the Mediterranean by means of a pipeline terminating in Tripoli, in the Lebanon, and Haifa in Palestine, but her Persian Gulf port of Basra lay close to the border with Iran and the vital oil refinery at Abadan. There was no military agreement between Britain and Iran, but in the event of threat to Abadan or the Iranian oil fields, the British could invoke the Anglo-Iraqi Treaty and land forces in nearby Basra. There was, in fact, a contingency plan, codenamed TROUT, to send one division of Indian troops to Basra for this very purpose, and it is interesting to note that the main external threat envisaged when the plan was drawn up in March 1940 was from the Soviet Union.

Summing up the position in the area at the beginning of July 1940, the British Chiefs-of-Staff wrote:

[3] John Connell, *Wavell: Scholar and Soldier*, London, Collins, 1964 (hereafter cited as Connell, *Wavell*), p. 232 (emphasis in original).

The security of the Middle East hinges on the defence of Egypt and the Sudan, where our main forces are based, our Middle Eastern communications are centred, and the Suez Canal is controlled; on the defence of Iraq, from which we must control the oil of Iraq and Iran and safeguard the route from Baghdad to Haifa; on Palestine, which is now [i.e. since Syria had declared allegiance to Vichy France] our most northerly defensive position and contains the western terminus of the Baghdad route; on Aden, which is essential to our Red Sea lines of communication; and on the defence of Kenya, which is our second line of defence in Africa, a valuable base of operations against Italian East Africa, and which contains a second alternative line of communication via Mombasa to Egypt.[4]

Aden and Kenya were never subjected to any serious threat because of the ineffectiveness of the Italian forces in East Africa, but it was a different story with regard to the other countries enumerated by the Chiefs-of-Staff, and to which must be added Syria. Moreover, the threat did not come solely from outside. The more extreme Arab nationalists, who had remained relatively quiescent during the 'phoney war', were given much food for thought and even hope as a result of the sensational German victory over France. One arch-enemy was down and the other, Britain, in a seemingly hopeless position of isolation. Before examining Axis strategy for the Middle East, therefore, we must look at the impact of these events upon the major Arab countries.

EGYPT

From the British point of view, the government in office in Egypt when Italy entered the war on 10 June, 1940 was far from satisfactory. The prime minister, 'Ali Mahir Pasha, had come to power in August 1939, and one of

---

[4] Archives of the Commonwealth of Australia, Series A1608, File H41/1/3, Pt 1. Material for this source will hereafter be cited as CRS (Commonwealth Record Series), followed by the series and file numbers.

his first actions had been to refuse the British request to declare war on Germany in September, although he did break off diplomatic relations. Moreover, the man he appointed as Chief-of-Staff of the Egyptian army, the veteran Arab nationalist 'Aziz al-Misri, had studied in Germany before the First World War and was a great admirer of German methods. The British authorities demanded his removal after he toured army camps telling the officers that Germany was bound to win the war, and he was given three-and-a-half-months' 'sick leave' in February 1940, which was extended by a further six months at the end of May.

But worse was to follow. The British government decided not to press Egypt to declare war on Germany, but on 25 April, 1940, when Italian entry was already looming on the horizon, resolved that if it materialized, Egypt would have to declare war on Italy. 'Ali Mahir, however, had different ideas. On 14 May he approached the Italian minister in Cairo and emphasized that if Italy did enter the war, Egypt would not declare war upon her as she did not consider herself bound by the Anglo-Egyptian Treaty to do so. The prime minister went on to say that Egypt intended to preserve and consolidate friendly relations with Italy, that his government recognized legitimate Italian aspirations to a share in the administration of the Suez Canal and to a proper status for Italian settlers in French-ruled Tunisia, and that it would never put any obstacle in the way of their realization. His policy was 'to affirm the personality of Egypt, which must emerge from the conflict freed from all bonds', and he looked forward to the day when his country, liberated from the presence of a foreign army, would be able to dedicate itself to forging links of friendship with other Mediterranean countries, to whom control of the sea must return.[5]

This was strong stuff and one wonders whether the

---

[5] *I Documenti Diplomatici Italiani*, 9th Series, Rome, La Libreria dello Stato, 1952 – in progress (hereafter cited as *D.D.I.*), Vol. IV, No. 412.

British ambassador, Sir Miles Lampson, got to hear of it, for we find him reporting at the beginning of June that the political situation was getting worse and that he was not fully assured of 'Ali Mahir's good faith. Once again, the British government changed its mind and decided that as long as military operations were not hampered, it would be better if a state of war between Italy and Egypt came about as the result of Italian aggression rather than British pressure upon the Egyptian government. However, diplomatic relations must be broken off and the Egyptian government must prohibit trade with the enemy and maintain internal security. 'Ali Mahir agreed to this and relations with Italy were formally severed on 14 June.

It soon became clear, however, that 'Ali Mahir was still hedging his bets. Although the Egyptian government had stated that Italian air raids upon Egyptian territory would constitute a *casus belli*, when the Italian air force actually proceeded to bomb frontier posts, the prime minister described the raids as border incidents which could be resolved by negotiation and told an applauding parliament on 19 June that Egyptian troops had been withdrawn a few miles from the Libyan frontier so as not to precipitate a conflict. Moreover, as General Wilson, the British Commander in Egypt, wrote later:

> The Egyptian Government adopted a very different attitude over the internment of Italians and the taking over of banks and business premises as compared to the previous September when dealing with Germans . . . During the preceding year our security services had been able to mark down certain meeting places and the most active agents. Though the police were most cooperative and often acted on our requests the greatest difficulty was experienced in getting the Egyptian Government to function. One met with interminable delays, and at times was faced with releases on the order of a Minister without reference or consultation.[6]

[6] Field-Marshal Lord Wilson of Libya, *Eight Years Overseas, 1939-1947*, London, Hutchinson, 1949 (hereafter cited as Wilson, *Eight Years*), p. 39.

Finally, despite the rupture in diplomatic relations, the Egyptian government was in no hurry to expel the staff of the Italian legation in Cairo.

In the circumstances, Lampson and General Wavell recommended an immediate change of government, and the former was duly instructed by the Foreign Office 'to tell King Farouk that the vacillation of Ali Maher [*sic*] Pasha was neither in accordance with the spirit of the Anglo-Egyptian Treaty nor representative of the feelings of the Egyptian people, nor conducive to the ultimate interests of the country, and that another Government should be formed.'[7] Dominions governments were notified that Lampson had been authorized to approach the Egyptian Opposition leader, Nahhas Pasha, to form this government, 'backed by the threat and if necessary imposition of martial law. If King Farouk suggests abdication, His Majesty's Ambassador is authorized to accept it.'[8] But it did not come to that. The king agreed to expel the Italian diplomats on 22 June and to dismiss 'Ali Mahir on the 24th. Britain had won the first round.

There was, of course, little that King Farouk, 'Ali Mahir, or his supporters, could do. The Italian foreign minister, Count Ciano, remarked that while the Egyptian prime minister's remarks to the Italian minister in Cairo were of 'obvious importance', their practical value depended upon the extent to which the Egyptian government could implement an independent policy. The Italian minister himself replied that no reliance should be put on Egyptian ability to pursue an independent line, for 'Ali Mahir had repeatedly told him that as long as there was a British army in Egypt, his policy was subject to continual hindrance.[9] A group of ultra-nationalist army officers, led by the present President of Egypt, Anwar as-Sadat, who planned a 'march on Cairo' in order to reinstate 'Ali Mahir, came to a similar conclusion and

---

[7] Woodward, *British Foreign Policy*, Vol. 1, p. 250.
[8] CRS A1608, H41/1/3, Pt 1.
[9] *D.D.I.*, Vol. IV, Nos 466, 501.

called off their attempt. The nationalists were not strong enough to overcome the concentration of British strength in Egypt by themselves. Only an Axis victory could provide the necessary conditions for a successful blow against the occupying power.

PALESTINE

The somewhat cynical view of the British government with regard to Palestine in 1939-40 seems to have been that while the Jewish community had no option but to support the mandatory power, (since a German victory would spell total destruction for the Jews), Arab support had to be purchased by concessions. The first step in this process had been the White Paper itself; the second was the announcement, on 28 February, 1940, of the land transfer regulations promised in that document and which prohibited the sale of Arab-owned land to Jews in two-thirds of the country and restricted it in most of the rest.[10]

When the regulations were debated in the House of Commons on 6 March, the Colonial Secretary, Malcolm MacDonald, was quite frank about the reasons for bringing them in.

> I must tell the House that we have had a most stern warning from Palestine in recent weeks that, despite the appearances, there was, beneath the surface, . . . a growing suspicion that His Majesty's Government were not sincere in their professions that they would protect the interests of the Arab cultivators, peasants and labourers, and that the population would become once more critical and hostile towards the Mandatory Power.

The Palestine Arabs, he went on, had kept quiet since the White Paper because they had been confident that land transfer regulations would be introduced.

[10] Jews were only able to buy land freely in 5 per cent of Palestine in an area comprising the central portion of the coastal plain, the municipal areas and the suburban industrial district of Haifa.

If we now destroy that confidence, the whole mood . . .
might well change. We might well find that the troops in
Palestine who have just completed their work of restoring
law and order have to remain there and start all over again
their painful work. We might even find that the troops
recently taken away from Palestine had to go back to lend
a hand in that work. If there was trouble in Palestine again
there would be repercussions in Transjordania, Iraq, Saudi
Arabia, and Egypt and even echoes of that trouble in
India.[11]

But Arab nationalists in Palestine and elsewhere were
not content merely with the introduction of the land
transfer regulations. Outside Palestine the greatest pressure for further concessions came from Iraq. To a considerable extent this reflected the presence on Iraqi soil
since October 1939, of the Mufti of Jerusalem and his followers, who had been forced to leave the Lebanon by the
French authorities. Although he was said to have crossed
into Iraq without permission, the Mufti was made more
than welcome in his new home. As Elie Kedourie points
out, 'he was voted £18,000 by the Iraqi Parliament, the
Iraqi government paid him £1,000 a month from secret
funds and he received two per cent of the salaries of
government employees; his men were everywhere, and
he became a power in the land'.[12] But Iraq's demands
were also a reflection of the country's own ambitions.
The Zionist leader, Chaim Weizmann, noted that during
the course of unofficial meetings with Arab leaders in
London prior to the publication of the White Paper, 'the
most intransigent among the non-Palestinian Arabs was
the Iraqi Premier, Nuri Said Pasha', and he ascribed this
to Iraq's support for a 'greater Syria', comprising Iraq,
Syria, Transjordan and Palestine, an arrangement which
would give the Mesopotamian kingdom an outlet to the
Mediterranean.[13]

---

[11] House of Commons Debates, 5th Series, Vol. 358, cols 445-46.
[12] Kedourie, *Chatham House Version*, p. 272.
[13] Chaim Weizmann, *Trial and Error*, London, Hamish Hamilton,
1949, p. 502.

It was in fact Nuri as Sa'id, now foreign minister of Iraq, who took advantage of the plight of the Allies at the height of the Battle of France to suggest on 25 May, 1940, that 'as a complement to the measures which the Iraqi Government were taking to defeat enemy propaganda, the British Government and, if possible, the French Government, should issue a clear and unambiguous statement guaranteeing immediately, or at the end of the war, the execution of the promises already given for the organisation of self-government in Palestine and Syria.' The Foreign Office favoured replying, with regard to Palestine, that 'so far as constitutional development is concerned, His Majesty's Government have not so far been able to regard peace and order as sufficiently restored for the first step to be taken, that is to say, for Palestinians to be appointed to take charge of some of the departments of the Administration. Nor do they think it likely that this step can be taken while the present war continues. But they hope and expect that when the war is ended conditions in Palestine will quickly permit the various stages of constitutional development to follow one another on the lines which the White Paper lays down.'

But the new Churchill government, and in particular the prime minister himself,[14] was much more inclined to sympathize with the Jewish community than its predecessor and the most that the War Cabinet would agree to (on 3 July) was a much briefer statement which omitted direct reference to the White Paper: 'His Majesty's Government do not see any reason to make any change in their policy for Palestine as laid down in May 1939, and it remains unchanged.' If British representatives in the Middle East were asked what this meant, they were to reply that 'His Majesty's Government hope and expect that, when the war is ended, conditions in Palestine will permit the various stages of constitutional development to follow one another in orderly succession on

[14] As a back-bench Conservative M.P., Churchill had attacked the White Paper.

the lines laid down', but the ambassador in Baghdad was told privately that 'there could be no question of promises going beyond those in the White Paper or even of defining the policy in the White Paper more clearly.'[15] Not surprisingly, this did little to satisfy the Arab nationalists, who were facing simultaneous frustration in respect of Syria.

SYRIA

Little of note had occurred in Syria and the Lebanon during the 'phoney war', although High Commissioner Puaux had taken advantage of war conditions to suspend the Lebanese parliament and constitution on 21 September, 1939, as he had done earlier in Syria. But the situation changed rapidly in June 1940 when, with the collapse of metropolitan France, the authorities in Syria and the Lebanon, together with those throughout the French Empire, were faced with the choice of whether to accept the armistices which Marshal Pétain's Vichy government had negotiated with the Axis powers, or to continue fighting. At first, it looked as though they would adopt the latter course. On 18 June, the day after Pétain's broadcast announcement of his intention to seek an armistice, General Mittelhauser, the French commander-in-chief in the Levant, issued an order of the day declaring that his army would continue to fight alongside the British, a development which the latter, as in other French overseas possessions, did their best to encourage by promises of support. Five days later, after learning of the Franco-German armistice, Puaux broadcast a message to the effect that no surrender and no weakening were to be envisaged, and on the 24th he sent a telegram to the French Resident-General in Tunis drawing attention to his decision to continue the struggle and stressing the need for the formation of a government in North Africa which would 'assure the unity

[15] Woodward, *British Foreign Policy*, Vol. 1, pp 559-60.

of direction and cohesion of the various parts of the
Empire . . . [and] maintain diplomatic relations in
those states not yet vassals of Germany.'[16]

It is interesting that Puaux did not see fit to contact
General de Gaulle, who, as early as 18 June, had begun
broadcasting appeals from London urging all Frenchmen who wished to continue fighting to rally to him.
One assumes that even if the French authorities in Syria
did not receive de Gaulle's broadcasts, they were notified
of their content by the British, and Puaux's diffidence
is probably a reflection of de Gaulle's negligible stature
at that time. In any event, de Gaulle himself sent a
direct appeal to Puaux and Mittelhauser on 24 June
which read:

> In full agreement with you on desire to continue war. Are
> forming a French national committee to bind togther resist-
> ing French elements. Request you personally to become a
> member of this committee. Accept expression of our respect
> and hope. On behalf of the French national committee,
> General de Gaulle.[17]

Even as this message arrived, however, the tide was
turning in Syria and the Lebanon against continued resistance. On 25 June Vichy's defence minister, General
Weygand, ordered all commanders in the French Empire
to observe the armistice. More significantly, perhaps, the
possibility of a link-up with French North Africa collapsed when the authorities there rallied to Vichy. On
27 June General Mittelhauser issued a fresh communi-
qué which stated that the Franco-German and Franco-
Italian armistices had brought about no change in the
status of the mandated territories and that he was
therefore ordering the cessation of hostilities. 'The
French flag', he concluded, 'will continue to be flown in

---

[16] Isaac Lipschits, *La Politique de la France au Levant 1939-1941*,
Paris, Editions A. Pedone, 1963 (hereafter cited as Lipschits, *La
Politique de la France*), p. 56.
[17] Charles de Gaulle, *Mémoires de Guerre*, Volume I, *L'Appel
1940-1942*, Paris, Plon, 1954 (hereafter cited as De Gaulle,
Mémoires), p. 272.

these territories, and France will carry on her mission in the Levant.'[18]

For a while the British Foreign Office favoured encouraging those French officers in Syria who were dissatisfied with this outcome to defect to the British side, but General Wavell was opposed to this policy. 'My view', he wrote later, 'was that I wanted a stable and neutral Syria on my northern flank, in view of my general weakness; and that to disrupt it by removing large numbers of the best French officers would be bad policy. It might result in disorder in Syria, which I did not want, and in Vichy sending out officers definitely hostile to the British to replace those we had removed. I did not think the gain of a certain number of French officers without units was worth the risk of this.'[19]

On 1 July, therefore, the British government issued a statement noting General Mittelhauser's order to cease hostilities. The statement went on:

His Majesty's Government assume that this does not mean that if Germany or Italy sought to occupy Syria or the Lebanon and were to try to do so in the face of British command of the sea, no attempt would be made by the French forces to oppose them. In order, however, to set at rest doubts which may be felt in any quarter, His Majesty's Government declare that they could not allow Syria or the Lebanon to be occupied by any hostile power or to be used as a base for attacks upon those countries in the Middle East which they are pledged to defend, or to become the scene of such disorder as to constitute a danger to those countries. They therefore hold themselves free to take whatever measures they may in such circumstances consider necessary in their own interests. Any action which they may hereafter be obliged to take in fulfilment of this declaration will be entirely without prejudice to the future status of the territories now under French mandate.[20]

[18] Albert H. Hourani, *Syria and Lebanon: A Political Essay*, London, Oxford University Press for the Royal Institute of International Affairs, 1946 (hereafter cited as Hourani, *Syria and Lebanon*), pp 231-32.
[19] Connell, *Wavell*, p. 241.
[20] Hourani, *Syria and Lebanon*, p. 232.

This last sentence, while reassuring Vichy, was a rebuff to the Arab nationalists. As the Australian government was informed on 4 July, 'the Regent of Iraq and General Nuri have urged British occupation [of Syria] which might well later lead to some kind of Federal union with Iraq, Egypt and other Arab countries.'[21] If this was the Iraqi concept, some of the 'other Arab countries' had their own ideas. Thus, the Australian government was told on the 15th that 'the Emir 'Abdullah [of Trans-jordan] and [King] Ibn Sa'ud [of Saudi Arabia] both have eyes on the throne of Syria, the latter for his son.'[22] It was also thought that Turkey might have designs upon her former province and Nuri rushed off to Ankara at the end of June in order to obtain an assurance that this was not so. For the moment, at any rate, all was well. Not only did the Turkish government consent to the British statement of 1 July, but it also agreed that any action under its terms should be taken by Britain alone.

Despite the extremely tense relations between Britain and Vichy following the Royal Navy's action against the French fleet at Mers-el-Kebir on 3 July, however, the British government would not be provoked into an occupation of Syria by the Arabs or anyone else. Dominion governments were told at the end of July that 'our object [in Syria and the Lebanon] is to ensure that the war effort should not be hampered from these countries, without having to tie up British troops. We hope to induce the local French authorities to prevent any anti-British activity or propaganda, to facilitate trade with Palestine and to cooperate in our contraband control. In the event of German or Italian attack on Syria we hope that they would resist it.' The authorities were felt to be amenable to pressure, partly on account of Syria's economic vulnerability, but also because 'the French position . . . would become untenable if we ceased to

[21] CRS A1608, H41/1/3, Pt 1.
[22] Ibid.

restrain the Arab nationalists or even gave them active encouragement (which we should not wish to do except as last resort).'[23]

An approach to Puaux was made along the lines suggested, but it met with a rebuff from Vichy. Economic-pressure was then applied, but it is significant that Britain continued to restrain the Arabs. When she did consider fomenting dissidence inside Syria in September, it was, as we shall see, not Arab, but Gaullist dissidence, and the Free French were no more sympathetic to the nationalist cause than was Vichy.

IRAQ

Iraq in September 1939 was ruled by a Regent, the Amir 'Abd al-Ilah,[24] and a government headed by the pro-British Nuri as-Sa'id. As we have seen in our discussion of Palestine and Syria, however, Nuri was a nationalist and pan-Arab in his own fashion and often differed from the more Anglophobe elements over means rather than ends. His cabinet contained anti-British members and was in any case dependent upon the support of the army which, ever since the Bakr Sidqi *coup* of 1936, had been the arbiter of Iraqi politics. Most of the army leaders were fiercely nationalist and anti-British. This was certainly true of Colonel Salah ad-Din as-Sabbagh who, together with three officers of the same rank, formed an influential cabal known as the 'Golden Square'. 'There is no more murderous wolf for the Arabs and no deadlier foe of Islam than Britain', he wrote in his posthumously published memoirs. '. . . If you give some attention to the location of countries and continents, and if you understand the strategic signifi-cance of the British wars, you will then see that the

23 Ibid.
24 King Faysal's son, Ghazi, was killed in a car crash in April 1939. His infant son, Faysal II, then became king. 'Abd al-Ilah was the child's uncle.

Arabs have no future unless the British Empire comes to an end.'[25]

When war between Britain and Germany was imminent, Nuri favoured an Iraqi declaration of war against Germany, but the more extreme nationalists and army officers wanted to extract concessions in respect of Palestine and Syria as a price for doing so. When Egypt merely broke off diplomatic relations with Germany on 5 September, 1939, the Iraqi government took the line of least resistance and followed suit.

At the end of March 1940 Nuri as-Sa'id was replaced as prime minister by Rashid 'Ali al-Gaylani. This seems to have been mainly a matter of domestic politics, and as we have seen Nuri remained foreign minister. But the change soon took on a deeper significance. Rashid 'Ali had opposed the 1930 Anglo-Iraqi Treaty and was much less inclined to work with the British than Nuri. When Italy entered the war, Rashid 'Ali resolved to play the same game as 'Ali Mahir in Egypt, and achieved considerably more success. The government decided, against British wishes, not to break off diplomatic relations with Italy and even began to insist upon qualifications to Britain's right under Article 4 of the Anglo-Iraqi Treaty to move troops through the country. On 1 July the War Cabinet in London decided to implement the TROUT plan and send an Indian division to Basra to help stabilize the situation, but both Wavell and the Indian authorities expressed the view that such a move might only make matters worse and possibly provoke the Russians to the north. The War Cabinet changed its mind and sent the division to Egypt instead, thus leaving Rashid 'Ali a little more room for manoeuvre.

Like 'Ali Mahir, Rashid 'Ali was also in touch with the Axis. On 26 June the Italian minister in Baghdad, Luigi Gabbrielli, reported that the prime minister had asked him to try to interest the Italian government in the fate of Syria following the fall of France. Referring to Nuri

[25] Eliezer Be'eri, *Army Officers in Arab Politics and Society*, London, Pall Mall, 1969, p. 372.

as-Sa'id's mission to Ankara, Rashid 'Ali told Gabbrielli that 'the Iraq Government is opposed to a possible occupation of [Syria] by Turkey and desires that the independence of Syria be recognized with a national government.' Ciano promptly replied on 28 June that Rashid 'Ali was to be told that Italian policy favoured 'the complete independence [and] territorial integrity of Syria and the Lebanon, and, moreover, of Iraq itself, together with other countries under British mandate.'[26]

A feeler was also extended in the direction of Germany. Accompanying Nuri on his visit to Ankara was the Minister of Justice, Naji Shawkat, whose purpose was to make contact with the German ambassador to Turkey, Franz von Papen. Shawkat carried a letter of introduction from the Mufti describing him as 'the person in whom you can place complete confidence in discussing the general questions concerning the Arab countries' and asking von Papen 'to convey to His Excellency the Great Chief and Leader [i.e. Hitler] my sincerest felicitations on the occasion of the great political and military triumphs which he has just achieved through his foresight and great genius.' The Mufti observed that:

> Palestine, which has for the past four years been fighting the democracies and international Jewry, is ready at any time to assume an active role and redouble her efforts both at home and in the other Arab countries. The Arab people, slandered, maltreated, and deceived by our common enemies, confidently expect that the result of your final victory will be their independence and complete liberation, as well as the creation of their unity, when they will be linked to your country by a treaty of friendship and collaboration.

He concluded by asking von Papen

> to discuss with my friend Naji Bey in detail the Arab question and the future of Palestine and of Syria, as well as the programme which your Government may deem

---

[26] *D.D.I.*, Vol. V, Nos 111, 133.

advisable to lay the foundations for bringing about the collaboration between our two peoples.

Although von Papen agreed to see Shawkat on 5 July, he emphasized, true to the spirit of the Axis, that 'the future development of the political situation in the Near East was a matter of interest primarily to Italy and that, therefore, I could be regarded only as an intermediary for proposals and wishes addressed to Italy via the Reich Government.' Shawkat replied that this was precisely the point. 'As the Arab national movement had fought Anglo-French imperialism, so it would have to oppose Italian imperialism. It was therefore to the interest of the Axis Powers for Germany to use her influence with Italy, in order to support a solution that would be compatible with the interests of the Arab movement.'

Von Papen argued that now they were about to enter the final phase of the struggle against England, Germany had a right to expect everyone, including the Iraqis, to make a military contribution. Shawkat was cautious on this point, but hinted that Germany would undoubtedly receive the support of the Iraqi army 'when the time came'. He urged that the first step should be the re-establishment of the nationalist government in Syria, terminated by the French in 1939, which would be followed by a resumption of the struggle in Palestine. He assumed (wrongly as we have seen) that Britain would shortly try to occupy Syria and an Arab uprising could succeed at such a moment of weakness. The condition for all this, however, was that Germany 'relieve [Arab] anxiety over a possible Italian imperialism.'[27]

Nuri's approaches to Britain had not produced much in the way of results. Would those of Rashid 'Ali and Naji Shawkat to the Axis powers be any more successful? In order to answer this, we need to look a little more closely at Axis policy towards the Middle East.

[27] *Documents on German Foreign Policy*, Series D (1937-45), 13 vols, London, HMSO, 1949-64 (hereafter cited as D.G.F.P.), Vol. X, No. 125.

AXIS POLICY

Arab nationalists were perfectly justified in suspecting that Mussolini's Italy entertained extensive imperial ambitions in their part of the world. This emerges particularly clearly from a document which Foreign Minister Ciano sent to the director of his armistice and peace treaty section on 26 June, 1940. Among other things, it called for the denunciation of the Anglo-Egyptian Treaty and its replacement by an exclusive treaty of alliance between Italy and Egypt, Italian instead of British participation in the condominium over the Sudan, and the establishment of independent states in Syria, the Lebanon and Palestine, all of which would be linked to Italy by treaties of mutual assistance. Iraq's status was left indeterminate in this document, but the German ambassador in Rome learned from 'an altogether reliable source' in July that 'Italy hopes to be able to conclude . . . a [bilateral] treaty with Iraq, too . . .'[28] To put it more simply, Italy proposed to take over the role of both Britain and France in the Middle East.

On the face of it, Germany was prepared to accept this. Commenting, among other things, on the von Papen-Shawkat conversation, the director of the political department of the German Foreign Ministry wrote on 21 July that in his opinion:

> There can be no doubt that we must give Italy absolute precedence in organizing the Arabian area . . . This, consequently, rules out any German claim to leadership in the Arabian area, or a division of that claim with Italy . . . All views about the Arabian area received here indicate a unanimous anti-Italian attitude among the Arabs. We ought not to allow ourselves to become involved in this Arabian game and ought not arouse their hope that they could get from us support against Italy.

The State Secretary, or senior Foreign Ministry official below the foreign minister himself, concurred in this

[28] *D.D.I.*, Vol. V, No. 114; *D.G.F.P.*, Vol. X, No. 193.

judgement. 'As long as we are still in the war,' he wrote, 'we should tell the Arabs only what we are fighting against, namely England, and only speak of the "liberation of the Arab world", without detailed reference to any goals for the future.'[29]

But there had been, and would continue to be, reservations. The above document was written after it had become clear that Britain was not going to throw in the towel and sue for peace as a result of the fall of France. In mid-June, when this was still a possibility, Ciano had been astonished and no doubt dismayed to hear the German foreign minister, von Ribbentrop, say that 'in the Fuehrer's opinion, the existence of the British Empire as an element of stability and social order in the world was of considerable utility. In the present state of affairs, it would be impossible to replace it with a similar organization. As a result, the Fuehrer did not want . . . the destruction of the British Empire. He asked that England give up some of her positions and accept the *fait accompli*. On these conditions [he] was ready to come to terms.'[30] In these circumstances, von Ribbentrop was loath to commit himself in support of Italian claims upon the British sphere of influence.

If Britain had agreed to seek a settlement, Italy could doubtless have obtained some satisfaction at the expense of France. But the British decision to go on fighting put a different complexion on that possibility. When Ciano put Mussolini's suggestion for a separate peace with France to Hitler on 7 July, he was told that one reason why this would be undesirable was because it would be impossible to occupy French colonial territorities, which would change hands as a result of the peace settlement, before they were seized by the British. The Fuehrer cited Germany's claim to the Cameroons as an example, but it was equally true of Italy's to Syria and the Lebanon. Until Britain was decisively beaten, it was best to maintain the existing armistice régime with France.

[29] Ibid., No. 200.
[30] *D.D.I.*, Vol. V, No. 65.

But how was Britain's defeat to be accomplished? In a memorandum of 30 June, 1940, General Jodl, the head of the operations staff of the OKW (high command of the German armed forces), outlined two possibilities: a direct assault on the British Isles, and '. . . enlarging the war on the periphery'. The second course of action could only be carried out by countries interested in the collapse of the British Empire, notably Italy, Spain, Russia and Japan. The most important measures in this strategy would be the capture of the Suez Canal and Gibraltar, thereby closing the Mediterranean.[31] Plans for German participation in an assault upon Gibraltar were put in hand in mid-July, while as early as the 1st, Hitler had offered the Italian ambassador in Berlin long-range aircraft which could bomb the Suez Canal. But the main thrust of German activity was to be directed against the British Isles, culminating if necessary in an invasion. Not until this possibility was ruled out did Hitler turn, and then only briefly, to a strategy which assigned an important role to operations in the Mediterranean and the Middle East. In the meantime he was content to leave that theatre to the Italians, although the Germans were well aware that while their allies might be stronger than the British in terms of numbers, they were weaker in almost every other respect, and that not much was to be expected from them.

In the circumstances, the German attitude to Arab nationalism was largely one of indifference, although Jodl's memorandum of 30 June did mention the possibility of using the *Abwehr* (the intelligence branch of the OKW) to give help to the Arab countries as part of the peripheral strategy. Even the prospect of gaining access to the Middle East's oil resources does not seem to have been the lure one would have expected, for Hitler and his military advisers were convinced that the war would be a short one and that existing supplies from Romania, together with the stocks captured as a result of the cam-

---

[31] Nuremberg Document 1776-PS.

41

Iraq and Syria, 1941

paign in the west, would be sufficient for Germany's needs. Indifference, however, is not the same as outright rejection, and the distinction between the two was more than enough to sustain the hopes of Rashid 'Ali, Naji Shawkat, the Mufti and their followers.

42

II

The Axis Declaration of 23 October, 1940

Nuri as-Saʻid was aware of the fact, if not the details, of the approaches of Rashid 'Ali and Naji Shawkat to the Axis, and seems to have tried to win them over by extracting the same sort of concessions from the British as they were trying to obtain from Germany and Italy. His opportunity came at the end of July 1940 with the arrival in Baghdad of Colonel S. F. Newcombe, a former colleague of Lawrence of Arabia, who had evidently been sent on a semi-official mission to find out what could be done to appease the Arab nationalists. It seems that not only Nuri, but also Rashid 'Ali and representatives of the Mufti, took part in the discussions with Newcombe and the British ambassador, Sir Basil Newton, which covered the whole range of Arab grievances, including Palestine, Syria and Arab unity.

A telegram from Newton, summarized by the Australian High Commissioner in London on 14 August, appears to have been the outcome of the Newcombe mission. According to the British ambassador, the Mufti's Arab Higher Committee would probably insist upon a solution to the Palestine problem which included 'a fixed date (irrespective of Jewish cooperation) for establishment of an independent government in Palestine', although 'Nuri . . . maintains that Arabs would be satisfied with promise to set up within definite period, say one or two years, shadow government under a king which on the precedent of Iraq would lead to complete independence within a period which need not be fixed.' In return for a settlement on their terms, Newton felt that the 'Committee should be required publicly [to] accept White Paper policy and to appeal to Arabs of Palestine

43

and other Arab countries for cooperation with the United Kingdom government.'

If it proved impossible to reach 'a comprehensive settlement', however, the ambassador proposed a number of 'subsidiary measures' of his own which 'would help to placate reasonable Arabs and diminish incentive or ability of others to make trouble.' These included the appointment of a few Palestinians to the control of government departments and some progress towards the establishment of an elected legislature, both of which would show that Britain was serious about self-government for Palestine.

Regarding Arab federation, Sir Basil reported that 'it appears that Iraqian politicians want to press forward with scheme comprising Iraq, Palestine (while still under mandate) and Transjordan and if possible Saudi Arabia, Syria being omitted in view of difficulties with the French government. Scheme would include extension of Anglo-Iraqian alliance to cover all members, currency union and removal of customs barriers.' The latter measure was somehow supposed to make the scheme more acceptable to the Jewish community in Palestine. The ambassador knew that the British government had hitherto been reluctant to make any public statement about federation out of consideration for France, but he believed that 'as a counter move against the Axis they might now make it known that they would regard with sympathy any move towards Federation which might be initiated by [the] Arab states themselves. In return they should ask for some public expression and tangible evidence of solidarity with the United Kingdom.'[1]

Although Syria was excluded from the proposed Arab Federation, it was not ignored. As the Secretary of State for the Dominions informed the Australian prime minister on 15 August, '. . . the Iraq government are endeavouring to secure the support of Ibn Sa'ud for the proposals

[1] CRS A1608, 141/1/3, Pt 1.

—(1) To warn the French government that unless they formed a National government in Syria relations with the Arab powers will be impaired and the Iraq government may cut off petroleum and/or other supplies to Syria; and (2) To request the Egyptian government to take similar action.'[2]

According to post-war accounts by both Nuri and Rashid 'Ali, the Iraqi government was prepared to declare war on Germany and Italy and send half its army (two divisions) to fight under General Wavell outside Iraq in return for a settlement in Palestine along the lines submitted to Colonel Newcombe. Indeed, Nuri is supposed to have travelled to Cairo to inform Wavell of this decision, which received no response from the British government. While there is nothing inherently implausible in the idea that the Iraqi government could have been negotiating with Britain and the Axis simultaneously in order to see which would offer the better terms, there are at least three reasons to doubt this version of events. In the first place there is no reference to the alleged Iraqi decision in available British sources. Secondly, there was no need for Nuri to go to Cairo for the purpose he described when there was a British ambassador on the spot in Baghdad. Finally, there was a completely different reason why he had to go to the Egyptian capital: namely, to sell the scheme for joint Iraqi-Saudi-Egyptian pressure upon the Vichy authorities in Syria, a mission in which, incidentally, he was unsuccessful.

In any event, the British government was not prepared to make any concessions to the Arabs on any of the issues raised during the Newcombe mission. In a circular to Dominion governments on 22 August on 'Arab Policy', it was stated:

> As regards Syria, we are discouraging any Arab policy likely to disturb the situation which has so far remained calm . . . In Palestine . . . the situation . . . remains such that we cannot accede to the Arab requests for general

[2] Ibid., A41/1/1, Pt 12.

amnesty, nor proceed to the first step in constitutional development laid down in the White Paper, i.e. the appointment of Palestinians to certain departments of the administration . . . In general since in the present circumstances it is not practicable politics to make a major concession, and since the value of immediate minor concessions appears doubtful we are impressing upon the Arabs that our policy is fixed by the White Paper of 1939 and the most we can do is to promise to fulfil it . . . The idea of Arab Federation remains as yet vague. We do not believe anyone can evolve a practical scheme, but we are doing nothing to discourage attempts. We would only be likely to intervene in order to secure our essential interests or fulfil announced obligations. We would, however, insist that any scheme must have the support of all leading Arab groups.[3]

Given the bitter rivalries among the various Arab leaders, this final condition virtually nullified any proposal for Arab unity.

In Cairo, Sir Miles Lampson was bitterly disappointed at the refusal of the government to make any concessions on Palestine. 'I have long felt something is stirring in the Arab world', he wrote, 'and . . . if, as I hope, we attach importance to keeping the Arabs with us, we should be well advised to consider whether we can do anything to meet them.' He believed that the Arabs were right in thinking that Britain was hanging back on the implementation of the White Paper and shared the view of Sir Basil Newton that Palestinians should be put in charge of some government departments, albeit 'with British advisers behind them to do all the work and all subject to the control of the High Commissioner . . .' But the Foreign Office replied that such a step would 'probably be found impracticable . . . under war conditions; particularly as Palestine may be closely involved in military operations in the Middle East.' Besides, it 'would arouse deep Jewish resentment' and the British government was not prepared to run

[3] CRS A1608, H41/1/3, Pt 1.

the risk of renewed racial strife in wartime. 'I understand and will say no more', Lampson replied. 'But do not let it be said later that I have not warned His Majesty's Government regarding potential nuisance value of Arabs if things begin to go wrong.'[4]

If British policy towards Palestine was unsympathetic from the Arab point of view, it was downright hypocritical in respect of Syria. Having consistently warned the Arabs against disturbing the status quo in the French mandate, we find the British government in September 1940 advocating a coup by the Free French. A number of factors prompted this move. De Gaulle's stock had risen sharply at the end of August when French Equatorial Africa and the Cameroons had rallied to his banner, and this, coupled with economic hardship caused by the blockade, resentment at the activities of the Italian armistice commission, and news of the unhappy state of metropolitan France, was causing some of the younger officers and civilian officials to contemplate throwing in their lot with Free France. The British representatives in Syria and the Lebanon urged that de Gaulle send a well-known personality to the Middle East with whom the discontented elements could get in touch and plan a takeover.

De Gaulle himself had set sail from Liverpool on 31 August with an expedition designed to seize Dakar in French West Africa, but on 16 September General Georges Catroux, the former Governor-General of Indochina, arrived in the United Kingdom to join the Free French movement. In British eyes he was the obvious choice to go to the Middle East and on the 19th Churchill filled him in on the details. According to Catroux's account, he was prepared to go if de Gaulle agreed and claims that the latter did so. It is clear from both de Gaulle's and Churchill's memoirs, however, that this was not the case and that the news of Catroux's despatch to the Middle East came as a complete surprise

[4] CRS A1608, 141/1/3, Pt 1.

to the Free French leader. De Gaulle fired off an angry protest to the British prime minister, who admitted sending Catroux on his own initiative, but emphasized that it was 'perfectly understood that he holds his position only from you . . .' 'Sometimes one has to take decisions on the spot because of their urgency and the difficulty of explaining to others at a distance', Churchill wrote. 'There is time to stop him still if you desire it, but I should consider this was a very unreasonable act.'[5]

Catroux was not prevented from going to the Middle East, but his departure was delayed by bad weather and he did not arrive in Cairo until 29 September. By then the situation had changed completely. De Gaulle's Dakar expedition had ended in ignominious failure, with obvious repercussions upon the Free French image. Moreover, the Gaullist sympathizers in Syria had been foolish enough to talk about their plans and had been arrested. Indeed, the Vichy government had sent out a special representative to investigate dissidence in the mandate and suppress it. In the circumstances, it was agreed that there was no prospect of the French forces in Syria rallying to de Gaulle spontaneously and that Britain simply did not possess the means to compel them to do so. Continued economic pressure and propaganda were the only way in which to induce any change in the situation, and there was still no attempt to enlist Arab support.

It is doubtful whether Rashid 'Ali, and more particularly the Mufti, ever entertained much hope of winning concessions from the British. The failure of the Newcombe mission, therefore, merely reinforced their prejudices and enabled them to concentrate upon their negotiations with the Axis. Indeed these negotiations were never broken off. Even as Newcombe arrived in Baghdad,

[5] Churchill, *Second World War*, Vol. II, p. 596. The hypersensitive de Gaulle had a strong suspicion that the British were grooming Catroux, who was nominally senior to himself, to take over the leadership of the Free French movement.

the Mufti despatched his private secretary, 'Uthman Kamal Haddad, on a mission to Berlin and Rome.

When he reached the German capital, Haddad claimed to represent an inter-Arab committee under the Mufti's chairmanship which included members from Syria and Saudi Arabia as well as from Iraq, but this was probably an exaggeration for the sake of effect. In a conversation with Fritz Grobba, the former German minister to Iraq and one of the German foreign ministry's experts on Arab affairs, Haddad explained that 'from Naji Shawkat's talk with Herr von Papen the committee had gained the impression that Germany was sympathetic toward the Arab aspirations, but that she would negotiate on the pertinent questions only in concert with Italy. That is the reason why he was sent now with instructions to negotiate first with the German and then with the Italian government.'

Haddad proposed that the Axis governments issue a joint or identical declaration on Arab affairs comprising the following five points:

1. Recognition of 'the full independence' of all Arab countries, including those at present under French and British mandate and the British protectorates in the Persian Gulf and South Arabia. This independence was not to be restricted by, for example, the establishment of fresh mandates.

2. Recognition of 'the right of all Arab countries to shape their national unity in accordance with their wishes' and the placing of no obstacles in their way.

3. Recognition of the Arab countries' right 'to solve the question of the Jewish elements in Palestine and the other Arab countries in a manner that conforms to the national and ethnic interests of the Arabs, and to the solution of the Jewish question in . . . Germany and Italy.'

4. Denial of any 'imperialistic designs' upon Egpyt or the Sudan and the recognition of these two countries' independence as in Point 1.

5. Expression of the wish 'to see each Arab nation enjoying abundant prosperity and taking its historical and natural place in the sun, both for the welfare of all

mankind and for the purpose of economic cooperation with
these countries in the mutual interest.'

This declaration was to be accompanied by a letter in
which Germany and Italy expressed their agreement
with (a) the Iraqi government's wish to restore diplomatic relations with Germany, (b) the Iraqi government's 'willingness . . . to accord to Germany and Italy
a preferred position with respect to the exploitation of
Iraq mineral resources, especially petroleum, and the
economic development of the country . . .' and (c) the
Iraqi government's 'willingness . . . to offer its good
offices . . . to achieve a like understanding with the other
Arab countries, especially Syria, Palestine, Transjordan,
and Saudi Arabia.' Once the declaration had been made
and the letter received, the Iraqi government would dismiss Nuri Sa'id and negotiate a secret agreement with
the German and Italian governments 'in which would be
laid down all the details of the friendly collaboration
envisioned'.

Iraq, Syria, Palestine and Transjordan would declare
their 'strict neutrality' and in the last two 'a general
uprising' would be started. It would have to be supplied
with arms handed over by the French to the Italian
armistice commission in Syria and would cost £30,000
in the early months, of which the committee could only
raise a third. Haddad claimed that such an uprising
would tie down the 30-40,000 troops which Britain still
maintained in Palestine and that, together with the
prevention of Indian troop movements across Iraq, this
would 'substantially relieve Italy's military position in
the eastern Mediterranean'. If Britain regarded the prevention of troop movements and the despatch of a German minister as a provocation and responded by force,
Iraq was ready 'to defend her neutrality against England
with all means' and 'to admit . . . all German agents or
experts necessary for the purpose.'[6]

On 9 September a slightly modified summary of

[6] *D.G.F.P.*, Vol. X, No. 403.

Haddad's proposals was sent to the German ambassador in Rome, who was told that the German government was prepared, in certain circumstances, to supply arms and money as requested, but that it would act only in agreement with Italy. The ambassador was to ascertain Ciano's views, particularly 'as to whether the operations contemplated by [Haddad] really have a chance of success.' The Italian foreign minister was sceptical. 'He stated that for years he had maintained constant relations with the Grand Mufti, of which his secret fund could tell a tale', the ambassador reported. 'The return on this gift of millions had not been exactly great and had really been confined to occasional destruction of pipelines, which in most cases could be quickly repaired.' Nevertheless, he agreed to have Haddad's proposals studied by one of his Middle Eastern experts, Giovanni Guarnaschelli.[7]

If, as he claimed, he had been subsidising the Mufti to the tune of millions for years, it is odd that Ciano had had to ask the Italian minister in Baghdad on 3 August for information on the Mufti's activities and his attitude towards the Axis powers! Gabbrielli had replied on the 16th that while the Mufti was 'the uncontested leader of the Palestine refugees', his authority and prestige were limited to this. Like other Arab nationalists, he hoped to use his solidarity with the Axis to extract concessions from Britain and perhaps to gain support for the liberation of Palestine. Only recently, Gabbrielli concluded, an emissary from the Mufti had asked him whether Italy could supply guns and ammunition, or at least the money with which to buy them.[8] It was probably this report, rather than his alleged long-term relations with the Mufti, which was at the root of Ciano's scepticism.

[7] Ibid., Vol. XI, Nos 35, 40. The Mufti of Jerusalem had been dubbed the Grand Mufti by the British administration in 1920 when it was decided to treat the incumbent of that office as head of the Muslim community in Palestine.
[8] D.D.I., Vol. V, Nos 348, 423.

This scepticism was reinforced by Guarnaschelli's assessment of Haddad's proposals. *'A public declaration recognizing the unlimited independence of the Arab states does not correspond to our interests'*, the official emphasized. 'Apart from other and more direct reasons, it is felt that free access to the Indian Ocean will never be assured if the Suez Canal zone, Sinai, the Sudan and Aden are not controlled by us.' Given the 'organic incapacity' of some of the Arab states to govern themselves, he continued, the granting of complete independence would expose them and their proposed union to the danger of falling under the influence of other powers. The Italian solution was to grant independence, but to restrict it with 'the simultaneous conclusion of an exclusive treaty of alliance and guarantee.'

Guarnaschelli also threw cold water upon Haddad's military schemes. The Arab countries, he argued, were occupied by sizable contingents of British troops and former Italian representatives in the area were unanimous in their opinion that the Arabs could not organize and sustain a large-scale revolt. Even Iraq did not have sufficient forces to prevent the transit of Anglo-Indian troops and defend her neutrality. Finally, Haddad's proposals were conditional upon the prior recognition of the unlimited independence of the Arab states. They therefore committed Iraq more than any other country, but were not put forward by a properly authorized representative of that country. For these reasons, Guarnaschelli did not think it was a good idea to issue the public declaration which Haddad had requested, although he felt that the contact should be maintained. The Mufti should be told that he would be granted financial assistance, not for a large-scale revolt, but for low-level sabotage operations against communications, oil pipelines and so on.[9]

While these consultations between Germany and Italy were in progress, Naji Shawkat turned up again in Ankara. Von Papen reported his 'urgent request that

[9] *D.D.I.*, Vol. V, No. 578 (emphasis in original).

the government of the Reich, too, associate itself in written form with the written declaration of the Italian government regarding the independence of the Arab states of Iraq, Transjordan, Palestine, and Syria. Only if there were a joint statement . . . could the Iraq government proceed to remove foreign minister Sa'id and to foment immediately new disorders in Palestine . . .' The State Secretary, Ernst von Weizsäcker, relayed this message to Rome for communication to Ciano, together with a request for the text of the written declaration which had allegedly been given by the Italians to the Iraqis. 'Please say', Weizsäcker concluded, 'that some sort of positive reply to [Shawkat's] inquiry seems to us advisable in order to prevent a defection of the Iraqis; [but] that, in this respect . . . we would be guided entirely by the wishes of the Italians.'[10]

When the German ambassador saw Ciano on 14 September, the latter dismissed the assertion that Italy had given a written declaration on Arab independence to the Iraqis as 'pure fantasy'. 'Being interested in the opposite,' he remarked, 'he would take care not to make such statements.' The foreign minister also read out and handed over a summary of Guarnaschelli's memorandum on Haddad's proposals. '. . . He said that the Italian attitude, as presented in the memorandum, met [German] wishes, in so far as it was not negative, but termed advantageous a certain compliance with Arab wishes, even if this compliance naturally fell short of these extensive wishes.' Once more Ciano emphasized that 'Italy had already spent millions on her relations with the Grand Mufti, without achieving any notable results.'[11]

In reality, Ciano was as mystified about the alleged written declaration as the Germans and he immediately telegraphed Gabbrielli asking him about it. The hapless minister was forced to admit that he had indeed communicated Ciano's pledge of 28 June[12] to the Iraqis in

[10] *D.G.F.P.*, Vol. XI, No. 51.
[11] Ibid., Nos 57, 58.
[12] See above, p. 37.

writing, before receiving instructions to the contrary. When Ciano's head of cabinet, Filippo Anfuso, saw the counsellor of the German Embassy on 2 October, he admitted the gaffe. As von Papen reported on the 3rd, this incident deepened the Arab nationalists' suspicions of Italy. Naji Shawkat had 'flatly' told him 'that it was impossible for him to return to Baghdad empty-handed. All the hopes of the Arab world were pinned on Germany. If these hopes were disappointed, the Arab countries would eventually do better to come to an understanding with the English régime.'

Von Papen's own view, which he did not communicate to Shawkat, was that Germany should look after her own interests and not bother too much about the Italians. If Italy was to control the Mediterranean and the Suez Canal after the war, he argued, it was 'imperative that the Reich should secure at least one land connection to the Persian Gulf independent of this maritime route.' Turkey had only gravitated towards Britain through fear of Italy and after the war would:

> again enter into an intimate relationship with the Reich. If, therefore, a safe land route via the Balkans and Turkey to the Persian Gulf is to be established after the war, dealing with the Arab problem . . . [it] becomes for us a question that we have to face. . . . The return of Turkey to a friendly relationship with us, moreover, presupposes the autonomy of the Arab countries . . . For this would relieve Turkey of her anxiety of being hedged in on all sides by the dominant Mediterranean power, Italy. This later danger would more than anything else drive Turkey into the arms of the Soviet Union.

Von Papen therefore considered it 'urgent that the Reich define – especially within the Arab movement – its economic and cultural interest in the Near East so that the hopes of the Arab world are not dashed even before the war has taken a decisive turn on this continent.' If the Italian government did not want a joint declaration on Arab independence, he concluded, 'the Iraq nationalists ought nevertheless to be told what the view of the

Reich government is with regard to the future shape of things.'[13]

There was, however, no immediate sign of von Papen's views being heeded. The Germans had indeed persuaded their ally to agree to the terms of an innocuous broadcast declaration on Arab affairs, but withdrew a suggestion to include a reference to Arab federation following an Italian objection that this would be 'ill-timed'.[14] Haddad, who had been waiting in Berlin until the terms of the declaration were finalized, was visibly disappointed when Weizsäcker gave him the text on 18 October 'While fully appreciating Germany's good intentions', he said, '. . . I must state that the Arabs expected more, namely, a German statement regarding the recognition of the independence of the Arab countries.' Weizsäcker replied that it was superfluous for Germany to recognize the independence of those countries which she already treated as independent, such as Iraq and Saudi Arabia, and she could not recognize the independence of the others until they themselves had proclaimed it. 'I do not understand', he said, '. . . how the Arabs could assume that Germany was somehow exercising reserve in making this statement.' 'The Arabs have had bad experiences in the World War', Haddad replied, and cited the example of the Sykes-Picot Agreement. 'The Arabs now fear that there is a similar secret agreement between Germany and Italy', he added. 'English propaganda asserts that this is the case.' Weizsäcker denied any such thing and Haddad then asked whether it would not be possible to inform Naji Shawkat through von Papen that the declaration was 'only the first step on the path of collaboration between Germany and the Arab countries' and that 'the further development of these relations is to be the subject of future conversations between the ministers of Germany and Italy in Baghdad and the Iraq government.' Weizsäcker agreed.[15]

[13] *D.G.F.P.*, Vol. XI, No. 146.
[14] *D.D.I.*, Vol. V, No. 688.
[15] *D.G.F.P.*, Vol. XI, No. 190.

The declaration which Weizsäcker gave to Haddad read as follows:

> Germany, which has always been animated by sentiments of friendship for the Arabs and cherishes the wish that they may prosper and be happy and assume a place among the peoples of the earth in accordance with their historic and natural importance, has always watched with interest the struggle of the Arab countries to achieve their independence. In their efforts to attain this goal Arab countries can count upon Germany's full sympathy also in the future. In making this statement, Germany finds herself in full accord with her Italian ally.[16]

In the Italian version, 'Italy' was substituted for 'Germany' and 'German' for 'Italian' in the last sentence. Both versions were broadcast, in Arabic, by the German and Italian radios on 23 October.

Apart from the declaration, negotiations were continuing over material support for the Mufti's proposed Palestine uprising. On 16 September Ciano told Gabbrielli that Italy was prepared to give the Mufti financial support for his struggle with the British and enquired how it should be paid. He did not mention weapons, but when Gabbrielli replied on the 30th he said that the Mufti had told him that the Palestine Arabs would require at least 10,000 rifles, 100 submachine-guns, ammunition, some grenade-throwers and dynamite with which to blow up the railway from Jerusalem to Al-Qantara in Egypt. He wondered whether the Italian representatives in Syria could not obtain this material from the French and hand it over to his men in Beirut and Damascus. Regarding financial aid, he would like it paid through the Banco di Roma branch in Baghdad. Ciano replied on 27 October that the possibility of sending weapons was being studied, but that it was unlikely that they could be obtained through the armistice commission in Syria. £5,000 would, however, be sent to the Banco di Roma in Baghdad as a first instalment of the intended financial support.

[16] Idem.

Axis dealings with the Arabs continued to have little relation to the overall conduct of the war. The Italian plan was to advance from Libya on the Suez Canal and the British took the threat seriously enough to send a third of the heavy tanks in England to reinforce Wavell's army in Egypt at precisely the moment when the danger of a German invasion of the British Isles was at its height. But Marshal Graziani, the Italian commander in North Africa, did not feel that his forces were strong enough to undertake an offensive, and it was only after much prodding from Mussolini that they finally crossed the Egyptian frontier on 13 September. Five days and fifty miles later, they came to a prolonged halt at Sidi Barrani, while the British executed a planned withdrawal to Mersa Matruh.

Meanwhile, German strategy was undergoing an important change. Originally Hitler had adopted the first of the two alternatives set out in the Jodl memorandum of 30 June: a direct assault upon Britain. 'Since England, despite her militarily hopeless situation still shows no sign of willingness to come to terms,' ran the opening sentence of his military directive No. 16 (16 July, 1940), 'I have decided to prepare a landing operation against England, and if necessary to carry it out.'[17] At the same time, he believed that the main reason why Britain refused to bow to the inevitable was because of actual support from the United States and potential support from the Soviet Union. The former could be kept in check by agitating the Japanese, but how was he to cope with the Soviet Union, which was, moreover, showing signs of wishing to extend its sphere of influence beyond the bounds agreed at the time of the Molotov-Ribbentrop pact of August 1939? The Fuehrer's answer was a lightning campaign against Russia, which would serve the twin purpose of knocking this particular prop out from under the British and of crushing the bogey of Bolshevism once and for all.

[17] *D.G.F.P.*, Vol. X, No. 177.

Hitler's military advisers, however, were not at all keen on the prospect of having to fight a war on two fronts. The army leaders believed that if it was not possible to launch an invasion of the British Isles in the autumn of 1940 – and the navy seemed to have doubts as to whether the necessary conditions would be fulfilled – it would be far better to concentrate on the Mediterranean, seize Gibraltar, support the Italian drive to the Suez Canal with German armoured units, and divert Russian attention away from Eastern Europe in the direction of the Persian Gulf. This was in essence the second alternative put forward by Jodl in his 30 June memorandum: the strategy of enlarging the war on the periphery. But Hitler was not inclined to accept it. At a military conference on 31 July he reaffirmed and expanded the existing orders to prepare for an invasion of Britain, and simultaneously announced his decision to deal with Russia by the spring of 1941. Proposals for the capture of Gibraltar and the despatch of armoured units to help the Italians in North Africa were to be examined, but only as subsidiary elements of the larger plan.

By mid-September the *Luftwaffe*'s failure to achieve the necessary air superiority over the Channel and southeast England compelled the Fuehrer to modify his views about an invasion of the British Isles. A peripheral strategy now seemed more relevant and there was no lack of persuasive advocates to emphasize its attractions. One such advocate was Grand Admiral Erich Raeder, the commander-in-chief of the German navy, who told Hitler on 26 September that 'the British have always considered the Mediterranean the pivot of their world empire', and that the situation there must be cleared up during the winter of 1940/41, before the Americans had time to intervene. To this end, Raeder argued, both Gibraltar and Suez must be taken, the latter with the aid of German troops since the Italians were incapable of doing it on their own. He went on:

An advance from Suez through Palestine and Syria as far

as Turkey is necessary. If we reach that point, Turkey will be in our power. The Russian problem will then appear in a different light. Fundamentally, Russia is afraid of Germany. It is doubtful whether an advance against Russia from the north will [then] be necessary. There is also the question of the Dardanelles. It will be easier to supply Italy and Spain if we control the Mediterranean. Protection of [Italian] East Africa is assured. The Italians can wage naval warfare in the Indian Ocean. An operation against India could be feigned.

According to Raeder's account,

the Fuehrer agrees with the general trend of thought. Upon completion of the alliance with Japan he will immediately confer with the Duce, and possibly also with [Vichy] France. He will have to decide whether cooperation with France or with Spain is more profitable; probably with France, since Spain demands a great deal . . . but offers little. . . . An advance through Syria would also depend on the attitude taken by France; it would be quite possible, however . . . Russia should be encouraged to advance toward the south, or against Persia and India, in order to gain an outlet to the Indian Ocean which would be more important to Russia than the position in the Baltic Sea.[18]

The plans for an invasion of the British Isles were therefore dropped in favour of the formation of a vast 'continental coalition', which, in addition to Germany and Italy, would comprise Vichy France, Spain and the Soviet Union, and which would concentrate its strength against the British position in Africa, the Mediterranean and the Middle East. There were of course immense problems in the formation of such a coalition. Italy, Spain and France had conflicting interests, which, as Hitler privately recognized, could only be resolved 'by means of a grandiose fraud',[19] and it was by no means certain that

[18] *Brassey's Naval Annual 1948*, London, William Clowes & Sons, 1948, pp 141-42.
[19] Generaloberst Franz Halder, *Kriegstagebuch*, Vol. 2, Stuttgart, W. Kohlhammer Verlag, 1963, p. 124.

the Soviet Union would accept the part assigned to it in the German scheme. These problems eventually proved insurmountable and the 'continental coalition' never materialized, which was probably just as well from the Arab nationalist point of view. If a strategy of direct assault upon the British Isles contained little of comfort for the Arabs, a peripheral strategy involving Italy, France and the Soviet Union offered even less. It was likely, for example, that France would have been permitted to retain Syria and the Lebanon as part of the reward for her cooperation, while Iraq lay directly in the path of the proposed Russian expansion, and Egypt and the Sudan still remained within the Italian sphere of influence.

As Hitler indicated to Grand Admiral Raeder, he would shortly attempt to sell the new strategy to Mussolini. The two dictators met at the Brenner Pass on 4 October, but what is most interesting from our point of view is not what actually took place at this Axis 'summit' conference, but the false rumour about it which reached the British government in London. Acording to the Secretary of State for Dominion Affairs, the 'Brenner meeting resulted in a decision to make a big offensive upon Egypt by way of Constantinople and Syria. The Axis powers realize that this would need months of preparation and it was probable that Libya offensive would not fully develop until eastern plans were ready . . .'[20]

This rumour, originally deemed improbable, seemed to acquire the ring of truth as a result of two subsequent developments in October: the despatch of a German military mission to Romania on the 7th and the Italian invasion of Greece on the 28th. On 1 November the British Chiefs-of-Staff produced a paper on possible enemy objectives in the Balkans and the Middle East. They suggested that Germany might be working to a three-phase plan, in which phase one would be the occu-

[20] CRS A1608, H41/1/3, Pt 1.

pation of Bulgaria, the occupation or isolation of Yugo-slavia and assistance to the Italians in Greece; phase two a German advance into Turkish Thrace, with bridge-heads on the eastern side of the Straits; and phase three, which would not materialize until 1941, an advance into Anatolia, Syria and possibly northern Iraq, which could be followed by a further advance, south-wards into Palestine or eastwards into Iraq.

While 'enemy penetration into Anatolia would not vitally affect our blockade unless [the Germans] were eventually in a position to draw large supplies of oil from Iraq', the Chiefs of Staff argued that 'the penetration of Syria would . . . threaten our alternative line of communication to Egypt via Iraq and Palestine, and our oil supplies from Iraq and Iran might be attacked from the air." Furthermore, 'an increased scale of enemy air attack from Anatolia, Syria or Palestine might affect the security of our fleetbase at Alexandria, and might eventually oblige our forces in Egypt to fight on two fronts.'[21] Thus was raised, for the first time, the spectre of a giant pincer movement against the British position in the Middle East, a spectre which was to haunt the War Cabinet in London and the commanders-in-chief in Cairo for the next eight months.

In reality, British fears were groundless. The Brenner meeting did not result in a decision to drive through Turkey into the Middle East – indeed, the possibility was not even discussed – while the Turkish foreign minister, to whom the British ambassador confided the rumour, correctly opined that the German move into Romania was aimed more at protecting that country's oilfields and firing a warning shot across Russia's bows than at laying the groundwork for an invasion of his country. We also know that the Italian invasion of Greece, far from being carefully coordinated with the Germans, was launched with minimum consultation and scant regard for their wishes by a frustrated Mussolini,

[21] Ibid., A41/1/1, Pt 15.

who was angry at the lack of progress of his forces in North Africa and suspicious of his ally's intentions in the Balkans.

It is true that some of Hitler's military advisers saw the very possibility which the British feared. The diary of General Franz Halder, the Chief of Staff of the German army, records one conclusion of a meeting at army headquarters on 26 October as follows: 'If something on a large scale is to be accomplished [in the Mediterranean], Crete and Egypt must be tackled simultaneously. To this end, Bulgaria and Turkey (the latter by force if necessary) should be induced to open the way to Syria across the Bosphorus. Perhaps a military pressure by Italy upon Greece fits into this conception.'[22] But the most Hitler would agree to was an operation, through Bulgaria, to seize northern Greece. This, moreover, had the limited objective of creating conditions for the *Luftwaffe* to neutralize the possible threat to the Romanian oilfields from the RAF operating from Greek airfields. Anything more ambitious was ruled out for the moment. 'We can only go to the Straits when Russia is defeated', Hitler told Halder on 4 November.[23]

Russia was indeed moving more and more into the forefront of the Fuehrer's thoughts at this time. The Soviet foreign minister, Molotov, came to Berlin in the second week of November and both Hitler and von Ribbentrop sought to persuade him of the wisdom of a policy of southward expansion. But the hard-headed Russian, though not ruling out the possibility, also demanded assurances regarding Eastern Europe. These exchanges evidently convinced Hitler that there was no hope of enlisting the Soviet Union as a member of the 'continental coalition' and the day after his final meeting with Molotov, Grand Admiral Raeder found him still inclined to force a confrontation with the Russians. Raeder recommended postponing the day of reckoning 'until after victory over Britain, since demands on

[22] Halder, *Kriegstagebuch*, p. 151.
[23] Ibid., p. 191. (Halder recalled Hitler's remark on this date.)

German forces would be too great, and an end to hostilities could not be foreseen . . . Russia, on her part, will not attempt to attack in the next few years . . .'[24]

Instead of Russia, the naval staff urged concentration upon the Mediterranean, and especially the eastern Mediterranean, an area which it argued was 'possibly decisive . . . for the outcome of the war'. Pointing to the failure of the Italian offensive in Greece (which had petered out within a few days), it concluded:

> (1) The German leaders responsible for the conduct of the war must in future plans take into account the fact that no special operational activity, or substantial relief or support can be expected from the Italian armed forces. (2) The entire Greek peninsula, including the Peloponnesus, must be cleared of the enemy, and all bases occupied . . . The occupation of southern Greece and western Egypt (Mersa Matruh) would considerably reduce the value of Crete for the enemy. (3) The enemy should be forced out of the Mediterranean by utilizing every conceivable possibility. In this connection the demand that Italy carry out the Egyptian offensive must be maintained and should be supported by Germany in every possible way. An offensive through Turkey can scarcely be avoided in spite of all difficulties.[25]

But Hitler was still not persuaded of the wisdom of avoiding conflict with the Soviet Union until Britain had, at the very least, been driven out of the Mediterranean. Admittedly, he made a small concession to the views of the navy. Military directive No. 20 of 13 December announced that the force invading Greece (Operation MARITA) would, if necessary, occupy 'the entire Greek mainland' as opposed to Macedonia and Thrace. But military directive No. 21 of the 18th stated emphatically that 'the German Wehrmacht must be prepared *to crush Soviet Russia in a quick campaign* (Operation BARBAROSSA) even before the conclusion of the war against England' and that 'preparations . . . are to be completed

---

[24] *Brassey's Naval Annual* 1948, p. 153.
[25] *Brassey's Naval Annual* 1948, pp 155-56.

by 15 May, 1941.'[26] Henceforth, the invasion of the Soviet Union was to be the keystone of Hitler's strategy and nothing was to be allowed to detract from its importance.

Unaware of Hitler's real intentions, the British had perforce to plan for those that were assumed, including a drive on the Middle East through Turkey. Apart from efforts to stiffen the Turkish will to resist, attention was focused upon Syria and Iraq. 'We shall most certainly have to obtain control of Syria by one means or another in the next few months,' Churchill wrote to the Foreign Secretary, Lord Halifax, on 12 November. The trouble was that there was little likelihood of a successful dissident movement seizing power from within and 'until we have dealt with the Italians in Libya we have no troops to spare for a northern venture.'[27] Gaullist weakness was underlined by the lack of response to a broadcast proclamation of his presence in the Middle East by General Catroux on 14 November, and on 8 December we find him dejectedly writing to de Gaulle that 'Syria is a bitter fruit which persists in not wanting to ripen.'[28] In the circumstances, economic weapons were all that were left. The blockade was tightened and all barter trade between Syria and Palestine was stopped.

In Iraq, the British resolved to take a firm line with Rashid 'Ali, of whose intrigues with the Axis they were fully informed, probably as a result of having cracked the Italian diplomatic code. Because, as was the case with Syria, there were no troops to spare for a military solution, General Wavell and the Chiefs of Staff proposed strong diplomatic action, supported by financial and economic sanctions. They also suggested that a special envoy, who was known and respected in Iraq, should be sent to Baghdad to try and steady the situation. The War Cabinet approved these proposals on 7 November and Sir Basil Newton was accordingly in-

[26] *D.G.F.P.*, Vol. XI, Nos 511, 532 (emphasis in original).
[27] Churchill, *Second World War*, Vol. II, p. 611.
[28] De Gaulle, *Mémoires*, p. 369.

structed to impress upon the Regent that 'in view of
Rashid 'Ali's intrigues with the Axis powers and pursuit
of a policy inconsistent with the Anglo-Iraqian alliance,
he must be eliminated from the Iraq government and a
new cabinet formed which will cooperate with us.'[29]

The Iraqis sought confirmation of Newton's *démarche* from London, complaining that the ambassador
had interfered in Iraq's internal affairs, but Lord Halifax
told the Iraqi chargé d'affaires that Sir Basil 'had been
acting on his instructions and . . . that His Majesty's
Government had lost confidence in the friendly good
faith of the Iraqi prime minister . . .'[30] Support for the
British position came from other quarters. The United
States minister in Baghdad, Paul Knabenshue, was instructed to inform Rashid 'Ali that his government was
giving Britain all aid short of war and that, as a result,
'any decision or action of the Iraqi government which
might result in a less cooperative attitude in its relations
with Great Britain could not fail to create a most painful
impression in the United States.'[31] Knabenshue conveyed this message to Rashid 'Ali and Nuri as-Sa'id on
5 December, while the Turkish government, worried by
the possible effects of an economic blockade of Iraq upon
imports through Basra, also expressed its concern at the
state of Anglo-Iraqi relations.

In a move palpably designed to force the issue, Nuri
sent a long memorandum to Rashid 'Ali and the Regent
on 15 December advocating a policy of cooperation with
Britain and the United States.[32] But the prime minister

[29] CRS A1608, A41/1/1, Pt 15.
[30] *Foreign Relations of the United States, Diplomatic Papers*,
Washington, U.S. Government Printing Office, 1870- in progress
(hereafter cited as *F.R.U.S.*), *1940*, Vol. III, p. 719. The Iraqi
protest incidentally delayed the despatch of the special envoy to
replace Newton, as it was felt that the latter's removal at this stage
would seem like a concession to Rashid 'Ali.
[31] Ibid., pp 716-17.
[32] But Nuri also appears to have tried to hedge his bets. The
Mufti's private secretary told the Germans in February 1941 that
'in December of last year, Nuri as-Sa'id . . . had told the Grand
Mufti that Iraq must work with the Axis powers; he himself was

was in no mood to listen. At the end of November he had appealed to the Italian minister in Baghdad to persuade Italy and Germany to denounce the British attempt to depose him over the radio, a request which was turned down on the grounds that such broadcasts might do him more harm than good. A few days later he asked for arms and ammunition, this time not to support an uprising in Palestine or some other part of the Arab world, but to enable his own supporters in the Iraqi army to stand up to the British. The latter in the meantime began to apply their programme of economic sanctions, beginning with a freeze of Iraq's dollar credits. There was even talk of expelling the Mufti, but Newton emphasized that 'no Iraqian government would face the public odium which they would incur if they were to surrender an honoured guest to his enemies' and urged that the problem of Rashid 'Ali be tackled first.[33]

By mid-December, therefore, the struggle between Britain and the Iraqi nationalists was well and truly engaged. It was to rage, virtually without respite, until it was settled by armed force some five and a half months later.

---

ready to cooperate with the Grand Mufti in such a policy.' The Mufti rejected this alleged overture of Nuri's, however, on the grounds that it was only a ruse to gain information about Iraqi-Axis contacts, which could then be passed on to the British. (Unpublished German foreign ministry records deposited at the Foreign and Commonwealth Office, London, Serial Number 647, Frame Number 255201. Hereafter cited as *G.F.M.* followed by the serial and frame numbers.)

[33] CRS 1608, A41/1/1, Pt 16.

III

Prelude to Revolt

Quiescent since the middle of September, the war in North Africa flared up again on 9 December, 1940 with the onset of the British offensive against the Italians. By the 17th the latter had been driven out of Egypt and the British forces, pressing on into Libya, captured Bardia on 5 January, 1941, Tobruk on the 22nd, Derna on the 30th and Benghazi on 6 February. The whole of Cyrenaica was now in British hands and the advance had covered 400 miles in two months. An entire Italian army was destroyed and 125,000 prisoners and hundreds of tons of equipment captured. Coming so soon after the successful aerial assault upon the Italian battle fleet in Taranto harbour (11/12 November, 1940) and the Italian débâcle in Greece (early December), the offensive in North Africa shattered what was left of Italy's prestige in the Middle East and gave a corresponding boost to that of Britain. It is a moot point whether General Wavell could have completed the job and driven the Italians out of North Africa altogether, for he was never given the chance. He was ordered to turn his attentions elsewhere, and in the meantime, Hitler, who had decided that he could not allow his ally to be evicted from Libya, sent the first units of General Rommel's famous *Afrika Korps* to shore up Italian resistance. Their presence and the other demands upon Wavell's forces more than redressed the balance.

The most pressing rival claimant for Wavell's attention was the Balkans. As early as 10 January, 1941 the Chiefs of Staff cabled Middle East Command:

Information appears to point to an advance by the Germans through Bulgaria to attack Greece, possibly starting as early as 20 January. . . . His Majesty's Government have decided that it is essential to afford the Greeks the maximum possible assistance with the object of ensuring that they resist German demands by force. . . . This decision means that assistance to Greece must now take priority over all operations in the Middle East once Tobruk is taken . . . [although] this need not prevent an advance to Benghazi if the going is good . . .[1]

Wavell and his colleagues believed that the German concentration in Romania, which was the basis of the Chiefs of Staff's anxiety, was merely a 'move in war of nerves designed with object of helping Italy by upsetting Greek nerves, inducing us to disperse our forces in Middle East and to stop our advance in Libya.' But even if the Germans did intend to attack Greece in January, there was nothing that Middle East Command could do in time to stop it and any attempt would merely 'lead to most dangerous dispersion of force and is playing enemy's game.'[2]

Churchill would have none of this. He cabled Wavell:

Our information contradicts idea that German concentration in Romania is merely a 'move in war of nerves' or a 'bluff to cause dispersion of force' . . . Hostile forces to be employed in the aforesaid invasion would not be large, but of deadly quality . . . If not stopped, may play exactly the same part in Greece as the German army's breakthrough at Sedan played in France . . . Is this not also the very thing the Germans ought to do to harm us most? Destruction of Greece will eclipse victories you have gained in Libya, and may affect decisively Turkish attitude, especially if we have shown ourselves callous of fate of allies You must now therefore conform your plans to larger interests at stake.[3]

There were even greater implications for Churchill in the Balkan situation than he revealed to Wavell. Recalling his thoughts after the war, he wrote:

Were all the Balkan states, including heroic Greece, to be subjugated one by one, and Turkey, isolated, to be compelled to open for the German legions the road to Palestine,

[1] Connell, *Wavell*, p. 310.
[2] Idem.
[3] Churchill, *Second World War*, Vol. III, pp 16-17.

Egypt, Iraq, and Persia? Was there no chance of
creating a Balkan unity and Balkan front which would
make this new German aggression too costly to be worth
while? Might not the fact of Balkan resistance to Germany
produce serious and helpful reactions in Soviet Russia? . . .
Could we from our strained but growing resources find
the extra outside contribution which might galvanize all
these states, whose interests were largely the same, into
action for a common cause? Or ought we, on the other
hand, to mind our own business and make a success of our
campaign in North-East Africa, let Greece, the Balkans,
and it might be Turkey and all else in the Middle East,
slide to ruin?[4]

Put like that, of course, the answer was obvious. But
was the problem correctly stated? We now know that
Operation MARITA (the German invasion of Greece)
was scheduled for late March, not January, and that
agreement with Bulgaria for the transit of German
troops was not reached until the very end of February.
This led to the deadline being postponed until 1 April,
and it was put back another five days when the anti-
German *coup* in Yugoslavia on 27 March, compelled
Hitler to include her in the plan as well. We also know
that Hitler was anxious to secure Turkey's neutrality
if at all possible, and that the entire Balkan operation
was, as far as he was concerned, the prelude to an assault
upon the Soviet Union and not the Middle East. But
although some of these facts soon became clear, the complete picture was not revealed until Operation BARBAR-
OSSA was launched on 22 June. It is therefore unfair
to dismiss Churchill's Balkan policy out of hand, even
though we must admit that the British commitment, first
to Greece and then to Crete, was to leave Wavell with
very little strength to deal with a deteriorating situation,
not only in North Africa, but also in Syria and Iraq.

Syria, moreover, was closely affected by the plans for
a Balkan Front. If Turkey were attacked, or entered the
war in some other way, Syria would assume vital

[4] Ibid., p. 26.

importance as a link between the former and the British in Palestine and Egypt. It would therefore become necessary for the allies to gain control of the country. But how were they to do it? The British did not have enough troops to do it themselves; they did not want the Turks to do it for fear of offending the Arabs in Syria and elsewhere; and the Free French movement in the mandate was, in the words of a Middle East Command appreciation of 4 January, 1941, 'virtually dead from repression and lack of internal leadership.'[5]

One possibility was to stir up the native population. The appreciation cited above noted that many tribal leaders, especially Druzes, had offered to cooperate with the British and, like most nationalists, hoped for British intervention to remove French control. Catroux himself had suggested that the best way of gaining Arab support was to issue a Free French declaration, promising Syrian and Lebanese independence with safeguards for French interests, along the lines of the Anglo-Egyptian Treaty. Shortly after the arrival of the new Vichy High Commissioner, General Henri Dentz, who had replaced Puaux at the end of 1940, Catroux told de Gaulle that he would have made such a declaration but for the following considerations: it would have produced 'a state of anxiety and possibly disturbances in the Levant, disturbances which we would not be in a position to calm down or assume control of, against which the army and the civil administration would join forces, and which would run the risk of being exploited by the Axis and Turkey. Moreover, General Wavell fears that while he is occupied elsewhere, a state of affairs will arise on the Palestine frontier which would compel him to withdraw men from the fighting fronts.'[6]

There was another reason for proceeding with caution. The British and Free French were in touch with General Weygand, Vichy's proconsul in Africa, in an attempt to induce him to join the allied cause, and it was agreed at

[5] CRS A1608, A41/1/1, Pt 17.
[6] De Gaulle, *Mémoires*, p. 371.

a meeting between Generals Catroux and Wavell and Sir Miles Lampson in Cairo towards the end of January that 'no definite conversations with the Syrian national leaders in Iraq are expedient until question of General Weygand's attitude is cleared up, as any attempt to negotiate now might provoke trouble against the present French authorities in Syria and against Weygand.'[7] What was true for Syrian nationalists in Iraq was presumably even more so for those in Syria itself.

In agreement with the British, Catroux decided to follow up the approach to Weygand with one to Dentz. On 31 January he wrote to the High Commissioner pointing out that Syria was facing political, economic and military difficulties. Politically, France had lost her moral ascendancy over the native population, which was turning to Britain, other Arab states, and even the Axis for support. Economically, the British blockade was biting, which gave rise to added resentment against the French authorities. Militarily, Syria was subject to Italian control and was in an unenviable position, sandwiched between Britain and Turkey. There was no immediate danger, Catroux went on, but the position could change suddenly as a result of Axis initiatives in the Middle East. 'It is clear', he wrote, 'that if . . . war flared up in Turkey, the lack of continuous communications between the latter and Egypt could not be tolerated. It is emphasized, moreover, that this condition [i.e. of continuous communications] would have to be achieved from the moment Turkey was attacked.' In these circumstances, Catroux asked, would Syria be prepared to rejoin the allies? If so, a secret agreement could be signed to that effect which would incorporate important advantages for the present régime in Syria, such as a guarantee of French rights in the mandate both now and at the peace, the lifting of the blockade, and a promise by the Free French not to rock the boat. This would not only eliminate the internal danger (i.e. nationalism), but also

---

[7] CRS A1608, A41/1/1, Pt 17.

the external threat, for Syria would then be on the side of Britain and the United States, which was bound to win the war, instead of following the dangerous Vichy policy of relying upon a German victory or a compromise peace.[8]

According to Catroux, Dentz told the messenger who brought him this letter that something might be arranged along these lines, but that the Vichy government had intervened. Given the High Commissioner's unswerving devotion to Marshal Pétain, however, this story seems unlikely. General Weygand also failed to give any satisfactory assurances and the British and Free French were back where they started. It was therefore decided, at any rate by the British, to play the nationalist card after all. Major John Bagot Glubb (Glubb Pasha), the commander of Transjordan's famous Arab Legion, records that '. . . in February 1941, we received secret instructions from England . . . to place ourselves in touch with the people of Syria, with a view to possible resistance to the Germano-Italo-Vichy government. Money was placed at our disposal for this purpose. It was agreed that Kirkbride [the British political resident in Transjordan] should deal with the Druzes and I with the Syrian tribes.'[9]

Meanwhile, General Dentz was having trouble with the urban nationalists and the Axis. The two problems were not unrelated. During December 1940 von Ribbentrop had decided to send another Arab affairs expert from his staff, Werner von Hentig, on a mission to Syria. The Vichy authorities were not at all enthusiastic and there was some delay in granting him an entry permit. Von Hentig's instructions were:

(a) To report on the political and military situation in

[8] Georges Catroux, *Dans la bataille de Méditerranée: Egypte-Levant-Afrique du Nord 1940-1944*, Paris, Julliard, 1949 (hereafter cited as Catroux, *Dans la bataille*), pp 91-94.
[9] John Bagot Glubb, *The Story of the Arab Legion*, London, Hodder and Stoughton, 1948 (hereafter cited as Glubb, *Arab Legion*) p. 307.

Syria and, so far as possible, the neighbouring areas. Does England constitute a serious threat to Syria by way of Palestine? Are the resources of France adequate for defence? What progress is being made by the de Gaulle movement? What are the methods with which English propaganda is operating and what success does it have? (b) To gather relevant data for our policy toward the Arab states. (c) To observe Germany's own interests of an economic and cultural nature and to report on them.[10]

Von Hentig was specifically asked 'to avoid . . . anything that might be construed as approval or support of any tendencies directed against the French government', but he seems to have disregarded this part of his brief. He arrived in Damascus on 26 January and, after presenting his credentials to Dentz, he energetically wooed local political and social leaders, showing them a film on the fall of France and reportedly inviting Moslem views on the formation of an Arab Empire, envisaging the convening of an Islamic Congress at Damascus and inciting extremists against Britain over the Palestine question, and by claiming that Britain had promised northern Syria to the Turks as the price for the latter's friendship. The British Consul General in Damascus reported on 1 February that the Syrians were excited by Hentig's visit and that the German cause had been advanced.[11]

There is no doubt that von Hentig's sympathies lay with the nationalists, whose interests he saw as coinciding with those of Germany. In the report which he wrote on his return to Berlin, he said that Germany was the only foreign country to which the Arabs could turn for support. 'English promises have deceived the Arab

[10] *D.G.F.P.*, Vol. XI, No. 626.
[11] George Kirk, *The Middle East in the War*, London, Oxford University Press for the Royal Institute of International Affairs, 1952 (hereafter cited as Kirk, *Middle East*), pp 87-88; Charles de Gaulle, War Memoirs, Volume I, *The Call to Honour 1940-1942: Documents*, London, Collins, 1955 (hereafter cited as De Gaulle, *Documents*), p. 92. (This English translation of the documentary section of De Gaulle, *Mémoires*, is used whenever it contains the original English text of a document.)

countries only too often', he declared, and Britain was in any case subjecting them to strong military and political pressure. As far as France was concerned, there was the experience of twenty years of French rule in Syria, 'which has brought what is possibly the richest country in the Orient to the brink of the economic abyss, disheartened and impoverished an enterprising and energetic population, and deliberately debauched an aspiring youth.' Italy's declining prestige and her record in Libya meant that there was even less inclination to deal with her than with the enemy powers. This left Germany, 'which has never coveted Arab territory or carried out anything but constructive and protective activity', and the Arab leaders hoped for German support for their aspirations.

General Dentz, von Hentig argued, had got off to a bad start by cultivating the minorities at the expense of the Arabs and by leaving the corrupt administrative system untouched. Oppression and British subversion were continuing, with the result that the inhabitants would to some extent welcome a British occupation merely to bring the existing exploitation to an end. All Frenchmen in the country without exception, von Hentig maintained, wanted a German defeat which would leave them once more masters of their own destiny. Dentz was prepared to defend Syria against a British attack, but 'a serious, self-sacrificing resistance against strong forces' could not be reckoned upon. No improvement in the situation could be expected, Hentig concluded, unless a German delegation was attached to the unpopular and discredited Italian armistice commission and Gaullist sympathizers in the administration were purged.[12]

Not long after von Hentig left Syria on 15 February, disturbances broke out. They were economic in origin, stemming from the privations caused by the British blockade and, in particular, from a decision by the local

[12] *G.F.M.*, 71, 50821-24.

authorities in Damascus on 27 February to increase the price of bread. But the troubles soon took on political overtones. The nationalists, led by Shukri al-Quwwatli, called a general strike, which quickly spread to other towns in Syria and the Lebanon. On 11 March the nationalists in Damascus presented the French delegate with a list of demands, including the restoration of representative government, which had been suspended in July 1939,[13] and the implementation of the Franco-Syrian Treaty of 1936. Dentz sacked the nominated Council of Directors set up in July 1939 and began negotiations with the nationalists, but as the French freely admitted to the British that they wanted to set up 'a puppet government which would support the military',[14] it is not surprising that they did not get very far, and there was a renewal of violence in the latter part of March.

In a conversation with the United States Consul General in Beirut, Cornelius van Engert, on 5 March, Dentz said that he suspected that German agents were behind the turmoil, a clear allusion to the von Hentig mission. Engert felt that this was a highly significant statement. 'I feel quite sure', he reported, 'that six weeks ago he either would not have mentioned the Germans at all or would have accused the British of fomenting the disturbances.'[15] Indeed, von Hentig's visit, the nationalist troubles and the despatch of British troops to Greece at the beginning of March seem to have combined to produce some kind of *rapprochement* between Dentz and the British. Thus we find Wavell and Lampson arguing in mid-March that the Syrian blockade should be eased because, far from inducing Syria to rally to the allied cause, it was harming pro-British elements and driving the country into the arms of the Germans, as von Hentig's visit had shown. Similar arguments had long been put forward by the United States government and it

[13] See above, p. 31.
[14] CRS A1608, A41/1/1, Pt 19.
[15] *F.R.U.S., 1941*, Vol. III, pp 689-90.

was therefore decided, on 19 March, to relax the restrictions on Syrian trade pending a wider economic agreement. There was also some back-tracking on the subversion front. Towards the end of the month British representatives in Arab countries were told that military considerations—presumably the transfer of British troops to Greece—required calm in Syria over the next few months and that they were therefore 'discreetly to discourage [the] present disturbances.'[16] One cannot help wondering whether this implies that they had played a part in encouraging them in the first place.

The Free French were very disturbed by this policy of appeasing General Dentz. On 30 March General Catroux cabled the British foreign secretary, Anthony Eden, to say that he felt that any economic agreement with the Vichy authorities should be subject to two conditions: 'the dismissal of enemy agents and the armistice commissions [and] the granting of transit rights across Syrian territor᾽ to allied troops.' Catroux argued that recent events had shown that Dentz did not honour his pledges to the Syrians and that it was unlikely that he would be any more concerned about those to the British. He pointed out that German propaganda was gaining ground in Syria and that Dentz was doing nothing about it. 'Some circles believe that the aim pursued by the Germans', he wrote, 'is to accentuate the disagreement between Dentz and the nationalists and then to step in as arbitrators in order to become the controlling influence in the Levant with a view to their present and future plans. This hypothesis seems very plausible to me.' Catroux concluded by emphasizing that 'Dentz's duplicity, his lack of character and submissiveness to Vichy can only favour our enemies and any agreement concluded with him must contain substantial political and military guarantees.'[17]

Dentz himself certainly did not seem particularly grateful for the British economic concessions. He told

[16] CRS A1608, A41/1/1, Pt 19.
[17] Catroux, *Dans la Bataille*, p. 116.

Engert on 25 March that they had made little practical
difference to his position 'because the present disturbances had ceased to be economic and had become purely
political' and reiterated his allegation that the Germans
were responsible, adding that they had been supported
by the Italians and the Iraqis.[18] On 1 April, the High
Commissioner came forward with a political solution to
his political problem in the shape of a broadcast speech
announcing the imminent formation of a new Syrian
government which would be assisted by a consultative
assembly comprising the leading figures in the political,
cultural and economic life of the country. A few days
later he appointed Khalid al-'Azm, a member of a wealthy
Damascus family, to head the new government. The new
head of government was a moderate and most members
of his cabinet had not been prominent in Syrian politics.
There was no representative of Shukri al-Quwwatli's
nationalist bloc.

This move, which was accompanied by similar steps
in the Lebanon, was unlikely to satisfy the nationalists
for long. Engert reported on 9 April that 'opposition
to the French is on the increase among all classes,
especially in Syria but even in the Lebanon.' Shukri
al-Quwwatli had told him 'that the people are not willing
to wait until the end of the war' – as Dentz had said they
must in his speech – 'before obtaining from the French
a definite declaration *re* Syrian independence.' It was
therefore likely that the extreme nationalists would
merely 'tolerate' Dentz's concessions 'as a transitional
arrangement to test the good faith of the High Commissioner. They accuse the French, with some justice, of
having done little in the last twenty years to promote
ordered and systematic progress or to create a responsible
governing class, while the French administration was
itself marred by petty corruption, intrigue and gross
inefficiency.'

Engert shared Dentz's view that the recent disturb-

[18] *F.R.U.S., 1941*, Vol. III, p. 692.

ances had been engineered by the Germans with Iraqi support. 'The Iraqi Consul-General in Damascus', he wrote, 'is openly boasting that the Syrian nationalists are "allies of Iraq" and that their policy and activities are directed by him. He is also reported to have said that the recent events in Baghdad all form part of same programme.'[19]

'The recent events in Baghdad' to which the Iraqi consul-general in Damascus alluded were the seizure of power in Iraq in early April by Rashid 'Ali and the army. We must now retrace our steps and examine the immediate origins of the crisis in Iraq, which was undoubtedly the gravest challenge to the status quo by Arab nationalism since the outbreak of the war.

We left the Iraqi nationalists in mid-December 1940 in open dispute with the British over the removal of Rashid 'Ali as prime minister. They were even prepared, or so they assured Axis representatives, to turn this dispute into armed conflict, provided they received the necessary arms and equipment and certain political guarantees. Early in January 1941 Colonel Salah ad-Din as-Sabbagh, the leading member of the 'Golden Square' army officer group, told the Italian minister, Gabbrielli, that Iraq not only required immediate military aid in the form of 400 light machine guns and ammunition, fifty light tanks, ten anti-aircraft batteries with ammunition, high explosives, anti-tank weapons and 100,000 gas masks, but also a new Axis declaration on the future of the Arab world, the formation of a national government in Syria, and an Axis guarantee of Turkish and Iranian neutrality in the event of hostilities with Britain. This move was followed by the despatch of the Mufti's private secretary on a second mission to Rome and Berlin. As well as another letter from the Mufti to Hitler, he carried a new eight-point draft declaration on Arab affairs which resembled the one he had transmitted the previous August[20] and which had eventually been

[19] *F.R.U.S., 1941*, Vol. III, p. 69.
[20] See above, p. 49.

watered down into the Italo-German declaration of 23 October.

Unfortunately, these approaches coincided with the British successes in North Africa, which, as Rashid 'Ali himself confessed to Gabrielli, 'naturally had a certain influence on sentiment in Iraq.'[21] The increase in British prestige, coupled with the growing impact of economic sanctions, in fact forced the Iraqi government to the wall. In mid-January the defence minister, General Taha al-Hashimi, proposed a compromise solution to the country's political dilemma whereby Nuri and Naji Shawkat, as the most committed representatives of a pro-British and pro-Axis policy respectively, should both resign from the cabinet. Although they did so, the Regent was not satisfied with this and demanded the resignation of the entire government. Rashid 'Ali, urged on by the 'Golden Square', refused to agree and even sought a dissolution of parliament when it seemed that opinion in that body was turning against him. The Regent thereupon left Baghdad on 30 January for Diwaniyah, about 100 miles south of the capital, where he could count upon the support of both a loyal local army commander and the Middle Euphrates tribes. The threat of civil war now reared its head and this seems to have convinced Rashid 'Ali and the 'Golden Square' that he should resign, which he did on the 31st. The 'Golden Square' had the last word, however, for they successfully insisted that he be replaced by General Taha, who, according to the British, was as much of a pan-Arabist as Rashid 'Ali, and who might even be working in league with him.[22]

The Italian defeats also had an important influence upon the Axis response to Iraqi appeals. Germany began to take a more independent line instead of bowing to Italian precedence in the Middle East as before. On 4 February von Ribbentrop decided that while Germany

[21] *D.G.F.P.*, Vol. XI, No. 601.
[22] This was perhaps a little hard on General Taha, who was weak rather than wicked.

must continue to display 'strong consideration for Italian sensibilities' in her Arab policy, 'in view of the fact that the Italians have kept the Arab question pending until now, we may, for our part, in the appropriate instances, take the initiative', although 'we should always let the Italians participate in time and let them outwardly take precedence.'[23] Three days later the Italian chargé in Berlin was politely told that since the Germans were now exploring the possibility of supplying arms to Iraq, there was no need for Italy to duplicate this work. It was also decided that Germany, as well as Italy, would give money to the Mufti.

By the same token, Italy was increasingly prepared to defer to German wishes. This was probably just as well, for the Italians were becoming even more cautious about encouraging Arab nationalism than they had been hitherto. This emerges very clearly from the Italian draft reply to Sabbagh's requests of early January, which was communicated to the Germans shortly before the fall of the Rashid 'Ali government. 'As far as armed help to Iraq is concerned,' the draft ran, 'Germany and Italy will only take on responsibilities for a serious reason and after careful examination. It is not their way and does not conform to the solidarity of their policy simply to make promises which cannot be kept.' In this connection, the draft recalled that Sabbagh had asked for the formation of a national government in Syria and an Axis guarantee of Turkish and Iranian neutrality. Neither of these requests could be granted. Germany and Italy would naturally do all they could to help Iraq if the later opened up a new front against Britain, but they did not want the Iraqi government 'immediately to adopt an attitude which would impel the British to carry out a military occupation of the country'. They would prefer the Rashid 'Ali government to remain in power and continue its skilful policy of avoiding a military confrontation.[24]

[23] *D.G.F.P.*, Vol. XII, No. 12.
[24] *G.F.M.*, 71, 50797-99.

No more encouragement was given Haddad on the occasion of his visit to Italy. Reporting on the discussions, the Italian chargé told Ernst Woermann, the head of the political department of the German foreign ministry, that 'Rome did not intend to put too much pressure on Iraq to take action against England. The area was militarily more easily accessible to England than to the Axis powers. Consequently an operation directed against England might easily result in an English success.'[25] There were undoubtedly good reasons for proceeding with caution, but the Italian attitude was unnecessarily negative[26] and gave the Germans added justification for assuming the leading role in relations with the Arabs.

Another important step in this process was Woermann's memorandum of 7 March on 'the Arab question'. Woermann wrote:

Seen in the context of the war with England, the Arab area holds a position of great strategic significance . . . [It] forms a land bridge between Africa and India. Vast numbers of troops and war material have been shipped in the east-west direction to Egypt, and war material to Turkey and probably also to Greece through Iraq, Transjordan and Palestine. There is a probability that now, with British troops released in North Africa, a movement in the opposite direction will also take place: Palestine and Transjordan as possible jump-off points for an English thrust toward Syria, or through Syria in the event of an intervention in Turkey. . . . Through these areas passes also a main route on which England and the Soviet Union might join hands, if the occasion should arise. These territories are of special importance for the air routes of the British Empire. Essential for Britain's conduct of the war are finally the oil fields of

---

[25] *D.G.F.P.*, Vol. XII, No. 68.

[26] Thus the draft Italian declaration simply stated that recognition of a national government in Syria 'is not in accord with the present situation.' In a conversation with Haddad on 26 February, Woermann took the trouble to explain that 'declarations concerning Syria were difficult because they involved the danger of pushing Syria into the camp of de Gaulle.' See *D.G.F.P.*, Vol. XII, No. 92.

Mosul with the pipeline to the Mediterranean . . .[27]

At the same time, Woermann did not believe that 'a *decisive* blow to the British Empire could be delivered in this area' except as a result of 'operations against Egypt and/or military occupation of the Arabian land bridge.' The region therefore lay 'beyond the effective range of the Axis powers *at the present time* – except with respect to the *Luftwaffe*. This situation will not change as long as Turkey remains neutral.' This did not mean, however, that nothing could be done. Woermann indeed went on to outline seven possible courses of action: propaganda, sabotage operations (as proposed by the *Abwehr*), the issuing of a political declaration on Greater Arabia, supplying of arms and ammunition to Arab countries, financial assistance, persuading Iraq to enter the war, and strengthening German representation in Syria as von Hentig had suggested.

With regard to the political declaration, Woermann said that 'purely from the standpoint of the German interests, there could be no objection . . . Given the Arabs' dislike of the English and of the Italians, it would certainly be easy for us to attain a position of influence in a Greater Arab empire.' But there were difficulties in respect of other powers, namely Italy, France, Turkey and the Soviet Union, all of which had interests in the Arab world. 'When all these factors are taken into account,' Woermann concluded, 'it appears to be difficult in any case to issue a declaration in favour of a Greater Arab federation, which is based on an accord with Italy and goes substantially beyond our former declaration',[28] although 'some kind of reaction to the wishes expressed by the Grand Mufti . . . would . . . be desirable . . .'

Arms deliveries were mainly of importance in con-

[27] In reality, it was the Iranian oil which was so vital to the British war effort in the Middle East. They could have done without Iraqi production.

[28] The draft Italian declaration cited earlier was described as 'so tortuous that it would be preferable to have it dropped.'

nection with Iraq. 'This matter has been the subject of
discussions between the specialist of the Economic
Policy Department and the OKW', wrote Woermann.
They had concluded that:

> neither captured English arms [the Iraqis were trained in
> the use of British weapons] nor arms from German Army
> stocks may in any substantial quantities be released with-
> out the Fuehrer's authorization. It will not be necessary to
> seek such an authorization, however, until the question of a
> route for the transport of the material has been definitely
> settled. Since the route through the Soviet Union must be
> ruled out,[29] there is no route except through Turkey. To-
> day, Turkey would surely refuse transit of shipments to
> Iraq. But since Turkey permits transit of arms shipments
> to Iran and Afghanistan, the question is now being studied
> of whether it might not be possible, under some
> camouflage, to add such shipments to those going to
> Iran.

The Iraqis had also been negotiating with the Japanese
on this matter, but the latter had broken off the negotiations after the fall of the Rashid 'Ali government. Woermann therefore recommended that the exploration of all
possible ways of supplying arms be continued and gave
notice that 'a decision of the Fuehrer may be requested,
once the question is sufficiently clarified.'

Woermann did not believe that Iraq should be induced to declare war on Britain at this stage. Not only
were the Axis powers unable to fulfil the political conditions laid down by Sabbagh, but 'given the present
situation and the facility for English troops to be moved
by sea, by way of Basra, and over the Arabian land
bridge from Egypt, open resistance by Iraq against
England could have only a brief success . . . In these
circumstances it must be our policy to keep Iraq's confidence in us alive through the measures discussed above,
so that Iraq will strike when the over-all military and

[29] This, apparently, was not because of the planned invasion of
the Soviet Union, but because the transport of munitions did not
come within the scope of the transit agreement concluded between
Molotov and Ribbentrop in September 1939.

political situation makes such action desirable.'³⁰

It is not clear whether Woermann was aware of German military plans, and in particular those relating to the invasion of Russia. But his immediate superior, State Secretary Weizsäcker, was. Commenting on Woermann's memorandum, which he found 'clear and valuable', he made the telling point that 'how the Arab movement is best to be exploited against England depends on the larger problem of Germany-Russia.' If there was no need to show consideration for the Russians, in other words if BARBAROSSA was to go ahead, Woermann's relatively modest proposals were the right ones. But, in Weizsäcker's opinion, 'only the entry of a hostile great power [into the Arab area] would be a menace to England; that is, the unleashing of Russia in this direction . . .' He believed that there were other good reasons in favour of this course of action, but it could of course only be pursued 'if military decisions of an entirely different kind have not already been made.'³¹

Apart from what can only be described as a bureaucratic veto upon the *Abwehr*'s plans for independent operations in the Middle East, von Ribbentrop approved all Woermann's proposals. As already indicated, these included a reply to the Mufti's letter to Hitler. In order not to over-emphasize its importance, this was signed, not by Hitler himself, nor even by von Ribbentrop, but by Weizsäcker. It included the following statement of aims, which had been cleared with the Italian government:

Germany, which has never possessed Arab territories, has no territorial aims in the Arab area. She is of the opinion that the Arabs, a people with an old civilization, who have demonstrated their competence for administrative activity and their military virtues, are entirely capabable of governing themselves. Germany therefore recognizes the complete independence of the Arab states, or where this has not yet been achieved, the claim to win it. Germans and Arabs have common enemies in the English and the Jews

³⁰ *D.G.F.P.*, Vol. XII, No. 133 (emphasis in original).
³¹ Ibid., No. 159.

and are united in the struggle against them . . . [Germany] is glad to cooperate in a friendly manner with the Arabs and, if they are forced to fight England in order to achieve their national aims, to grant them military and financial assistance in so far as is possible. In order to assist the Arabs in their preparations for a possible struggle against England, Germany is also prepared to supply them with war material at once, in so far as a route for transporting it can be found.[32]

This letter was dated 8 April, 1941 and it was not handed over to the Hungarian Legation in Ankara for transmission to the Iraqis until the 16th. It was already out of date when it was signed, however, for circumstances had compelled the 'Golden Square' to mount a *coup* against the Taha government on 2 April. Now in open rebellion against the British, the Iraqi nationalists required more than promises to see them through.

What had happened was this: during the first week in March, General Taha's foreign minister, Tawfiq as-Suwaydi, was summoned to Cairo to meet the British foreign secretary. According to the official history of British foreign policy:

> Mr Eden said that Great Britain required a more cooperative attitude, and in particular, the immediate breaking off of relations with Italy. The [Iraqi] foreign minister seemed willing to agree, but explained the difficulty of getting the cooperation of the army. He said that since the beginning of the war Great Britain had kept the Iraqi army short of war material, and that it had become more difficult to break with Italy at our request. If he were given time he would try to win over the army leaders; otherwise he would attempt to remove them. If he failed to to so he would resign.[33]

To judge from a private letter from General Sir John Dill, the Chief of the Imperial General Staff, who accompanied Eden on his mission to the Middle East, the British had precious little faith in these assurances. 'We have had that nasty little red fox, Tawfiq as-Suwaydi, . . .

[32] *D.G.F.P.*, Vol. XII, No. 292.
[33] Woodward, *British Foreign Policy*, Vol. I, p. 573.

over here', he wrote. 'He has been all honeyed words but is obviously quite unreliable.'[34] In reality, however, when the Iraqi foreign minister returned to Baghdad on 17 March, he persuaded General Taha, albeit with the help of some pressure from the Regent, to move against the 'Golden Square'. The latter responded by calling out their forces to overthrow the government. They intended to arrest the Regent, but he got wind of the plot and turned up at the American Legation on the morning of 2 April, disguised as a woman. He was then smuggled out to the RAF base at Habbaniya hidden under a rug in the back seat of the minister's car. After an unsuccessful attempt to organize resistance in Basra, he left for Amman, the capital of his uncle, the Amir 'Abdullah of Transjordan. Rashid 'Ali, meanwhile, was appointed head of a new 'government of national defence' on 3 April.

Although the situation in Iraq had been threatening to erupt into crisis for some time, the *coup* itself seems to have caught everyone by surprise. On the British side, discussions concerning contingency plans for military intervention had been going on between Middle East Command, India Command and the War Office since February. Interestingly enough, the initiative had come from India Command, where the commander-in-chief, General Auchinleck, took the view that 'the sooner we begin to get control, militarily, in Iraq the better.'[35] But although it had been agreed that initial control of any operations should rest with India, no agreement had been reached on the plan to be followed. British diplomacy was also caught on the wrong foot by the *coup*, for Sir Basil Newton's successor, Sir Kinahan Cornwallis, arrived in Baghdad on the very day of the Regent's hasty depart-ure.[36] On the Axis side, enough evidence has already

[34] John Connell, *Auchinleck*, London, Cassell, 1959 (hereafter cited as Connell, *Auchinleck*), p. 197.
[35] Connell, *Auchinleck*, p. 198.
[36] It should be pointed out, however, that Cornwallis was not a stranger to Iraq, having served as an adviser to the Ministry of the Interior from 1921 to 1935.

been quoted to show that neither Germany nor Italy was anxious for the Iraqis to provoke a military confrontation with the British until they were in a position to win it. This could hardly be said to be the case at the beginning of April 1941. The response of both sides to the Rashid 'Ali *coup* was therefore bound to be in the nature of an improvisation. It was perhaps fortunate for the British that this was a realm in which they were traditionally supposed to excel.

IV

The Campaign in Iraq

The Iraqi *coup* could hardly have come at a worse time for the British, for it occurred almost simultaneously with the onset of Rommel's counter-offensive in North Africa and the German invasion of Yugoslavia and Greece. Indeed, some thought the three events were closely inter-related. The Joint Planning Staff of the British Chiefs of Staff believed that the North African and Balkan operations were part of a coordinated plan, while the newly arrived British ambassador in Baghdad, Sir Kinahan Cornwallis, agreed with the United States minister that the revolt in Iraq had been deliberately timed to coincide with the German attack upon Yugoslavia and Greece. In fact, none of this was true. Rommel's orders were essentially defensive and his lightning advance was carried out on his own initiative, much to the annoyance of his superiors in the army high command; and we have already seen that the Iraqi *coup* was precipitated by a British move (the Eden-Suwaydi conversation) and not by orders from Rome or Berlin.

Nevertheless, it is essential to give a brief chronological outline of what happened in North Africa and the Balkans during the month of April, 1941, as this formed the background against which the War Cabinet in London and the harassed commanders in the Middle East, particularly General Wavell, had to make a decision about Iraq.

Rommel's forces captured Mersa Brega on 1 April. This was followed, on the 3rd, by the capture of Benghazi, and on the 7th, by that of Derna. By the 13th British forces had been completely driven out of Libya with the exception of Tobruk, which was encircled on the land side by the Axis. Rommel launched the first of several assaults on the town on 15 April, but it failed. The invasion of Yugoslavia and Greece began on 6

April. On the 8th the Germans captured Salonika and
on the 13th Belgrade. The Yugoslav armed forces capitu-
lated on 17 April and those of Greece in Epirus and
Macedonia followed suit on the 20th. On the following
day the British government agreed to a Greek request to
withdraw its forces from the mainland and the evacuation was completed by 30 April. Anglo-Greek resistance
was now centred upon the island of Crete.

In spite of these pressing problems elsewhere, the
British government was determined not to neglect or
ignore the situation in Iraq. On 4 April the Chiefs of
Staff asked Wavell how many troops he could spare for
Iraq, while the Foreign Office enquired of Cornwallis
about the prospects of successful resistance to Rashid
'Ali. The ambassador replied on the following day.
Bearing in mind that Rashid 'Ali's status was unconsti-
tutional – he had been nominated by the army and not
by the Regent – he argued that there were three possible
courses of action: (1) to overthrow the new government
by force; (2) to refuse to recognize it and to try and
squeeze Rashid 'Ali; (3) to recognize the new government. Cornwallis felt that the third alternative was un-
thinkable and advocated the first, provided the necessary troops could be spared.

But here was the rub. On 7 April Wavell replied to
the Chiefs of Staff that, as a result of the critical situation in Libya and the Balkans, he could spare hardly any
forces from his command for Iraq, although, in a dire
emergency, he would move one battalion from Palestine to defend the RAF base at Habbaniya. He believed
that the Regent's position could be restored by a firm
British declaration of support together with an aerial
demonstration by the RAF units in Iraq. But should these
measures fail, he could offer no alternative solution.

Frustrated in its appeal to Wavell, London turned to
the neighbouring India Command. 'Some time ago',
Churchill wrote to the Secretary of State for India, 'you
suggested that you might be able to spare another division from the frontier troops for the Middle East. The

situation in Iraq has turned sour. We must make sure of Basra, as the Americans are increasingly keen on a great air assembling base being formed there to which they could deliver direct. This plan seems of high importance in view of the undoubted eastern trend of the war. I am telling the Chiefs of Staff that you will look into these possibilities.'[1] On the same day, 8 April, the Joint Planning Staff formally recommended that all possible steps be taken to overthrow Rashid 'Ali and that India be asked to send a force to Basra.

In reply, the Indian authorities offered to divert a convoy, originally intended for Malaya and which was at that moment embarking at Karachi, to Iraq. This comprised one infantry brigade and one field regiment plus ancillary troops. They also proposed to send 400 infantrymen by air to help secure the RAF base at Shaiba. They were strongly of the opinion that the land force in and around Basra should be increased to one full division as soon as possible and therefore proposed to follow up the first brigade group with two more. 'His Majesty's Government appreciates your immediate and most effective response to their urgent request for help in Iraq', the Secretary of State for India cabled the Viceroy on 10 April, 'and they gratefully accept your offer. Proceed at once with the despatch of force to Basra and Shaiba as you propose.'[2] The Indian offer was all the more welcome as Wavell had now come to the conclusion that he could not even spare the solitary Palestine battalion he had promised in the event of an emergency.

At this point, however, there was a sudden change in the attitude of Cornwallis. In an attempt to acquire legitimacy, Rashid 'Ali recalled the Iraqi parliament on 10 April and persuaded it to choose a new Regent, Sharif Sharaf, a distinguished veteran of the First World War Arab Revolt and a distant relative of the Hashimite family. Technically, this was as illegal as any of Rashid 'Ali's other actions, but the fact that he had been able to

[1] Churchill, *Second World War*, Vol. III, p. 225.
[2] Connell, *Auchinleck*, p. 201.

get away with it indicated that he was consolidating his hold over the country and that there was no widespread enthusiasm for the legal Regent, 'Abd al-Ilah. Rashid 'Ali also delivered a very clever speech to parliament which included a statement to the effect that the new government intended to honour its obligations under the Anglo-Iraqi Treaty. The ambassador reported on 11 April that this statement deprived the British of their best excuse for landing Indian troops at Basra, namely, in order to protect their treaty rights, and he proposed that Rashid 'Ali's good faith be tested by informing him that the situation outside Iraq required the despatch of troops through the country under Article 4 of the Treaty and that they would arrive on a date to be decided. If the prime minister agreed, the British would gain a foothold in Iraq peacefully. If on the other hand he refused, they would then have the justification to take any action they saw fit. In the meantime, however, the arrival of the Indian troops should be deferred pending the approach to Rashid 'Ali.

Cornwallis's argument was accepted and on 12 April the Chiefs of Staff instructed India that the departure of the airborne troops for Shaiba should be suspended and that the convoy, which had already set sail, should be held up at Bahrein or some other point en route. General Auchinleck, the commander-in-chief in India, was not at all happy with this decision. 'My own opinion', he wrote to the Viceroy's private secretary, 'is that the acceptance of the ambassador's advice to defer action for the securing of Basra may very well result in our never getting Basra at all.' He was 'convinced . . . that the possession of a base at Basra may make the difference between success and failure to us in the Near and Middle East during the next six months' and felt that 'the time for diplomatic parleying has passed.' There was 'a very definite danger that Rashid will use the breathing space Cornwallis proposes to consolidate his position and, probably, to invoke German aid, which might even take the form of airborne troops and aircraft. I am convinced that, if we are to prevent a general deterioration of the situation in Asia generally, and especially in Turkey, Iran, Iraq and Arabia, we must show now that we are prepared to maintain our position by force.'[3]

Lord Linlithgow, the Viceroy, enthusiastically relayed Auchinleck's comments to London. He also added some of his own:

> We cannot dump troops in Bahrein or Kuwait without showing our hand and giving Axis powers excuse for intervening in aid of Rashid 'Ali. . . . While decision must be for H.M.G. with their acquaintance with the whole picture, I feel no doubt myself that the definite line is the wise one. I express no view as to whether we have not been much too tender over the pre-war period with Iraq, from which we have had no cooperation that has mattered, and which essentially owes her existence to us. But we are moving into a position that affects our general standing in the Middle East, that has most important potential repercussions on India and Iran, that affects our oil supplies (so vital to the Admiralty) in Iran and in Bahrein (and to a lesser extent Kuwait); and I have no doubt that we must be prepared to take a strong line now.[4]

These representations from India carried the day and on 13 April the Defence Committee of the War Cabinet reversed the earlier decision and resolved that the Basra expedition should proceed as originally planned. On the evening of the 16th Cornwallis told Rashid 'Ali that the British government intended to avail itself of the facilities granted under the Anglo-Iraqi Treaty for the passage of troops and that a force would shortly be disembarking at Basra. Surprisingly, Rashid 'Ali took the news quite well. He may have been mollified by Cornwallis's hint that if his government fulfilled its obligations, there was a chance Britain might recognize it, although it is more likely that he was counting on imminent Axis support to help him drive the British out. In any event, the disembarkation of the Indian troops was completed on

[3] Connell, *Auchinleck*, p. 203.
[4] Ibid., p. 205.

19 April and during the same week the promised 400 airborne troops were flown from Karachi to Shaiba.

By 18 April there were signs that Rashid 'Ali (or his military backers) were having second thoughts. Cornwallis reported that it was already clear 'that Iraqi government is likely to prolong trouble and that army leaders having been caught by surprise will now do everything they can to nullify our initial advantage.' Rashid 'Ali had in fact forwarded

> the following wishes or requests which were originated by army commander: (i) Our troops should be moved through to Palestine at once. (ii) Other troops should not arrive until after their departure. (iii) In future more notice may [*sic.* should?] be given. (iv) Troops should arrive in such a manner that they can pass through quickly (i.e., presumambly in small contingents). He has also sent a message that Iraqi government consider it important that at no time should there be any large concentration of British troops in the country.[5]

These Iraqi 'wishes or requests', which were soon to be communicated in a formal note, were dismissed out of hand by Churchill. 'No undertakings can be given that troops will be . . . moved through to Palestine,' he told Eden on 20 April, 'and the right to require such undertakings should not be recognized in respect of a government which has in itself usurped power by a *coup d'état*, or in a country where our treaty rights have so long been frustrated in the spirit.' Cornwallis, indeed, 'should not . . . entangle himself by explanations.'[6] This hard line was incorporated into Foreign Office instructions to the ambassador two days later, although a little sugar was added to sweeten the pill in the shape of granting Cornwallis permission 'to express the hope that further cooperation by the Iraq authorities may provide evidence of their desire to fulfil the alliance and thereby allow the establishment of formal relations.'[7]

[5] Connell, *Auchinleck,* pp 207-08.
[6] Churchill, *Second World War,* Vol. III, p. 226.
[7] CRS A1608, A41/1/1, Pt 20.

The Iraqis were not, however, taken in by this ruse. When Cornwallis informed Rashid 'Ali on 28 April of the imminent arrival of the second batch of Indian troops at Basra, the prime minister, possibly emboldened by news of the enforced British evacuation from Greece, refused them permission to land. The ambassador was sufficiently alarmed by Rashid 'Ali's reaction to order the evacuation of British dependants from Baghdad. The Indian troops landed without incident, but the Iraqi high command ordered an estimated two infantry brigades with supporting artillery and mechanized units to occupy the heights overlooking Habbaniya air base. The Iraqi commander informed his British counterpart on 30 April that if any aircraft or armoured car attempted to leave the base, it would be fired upon. After obtaining authorization from London, the British commander, Air Vice-Marshal Smart, ordered his aircraft to launch a pre-emptive strike against the Iraqi positions at dawn on 2 May. Hostilities had now begun.

Although the 'Golden Square' and Rashid 'Ali had not engineered their *coup* on Axis instructions, they were confident of Axis support. On 10 April Gabbrielli reported from Baghdad that

> the victorious advance of the Axis armies on the Balkan and Libyan front is seen here as evidence that the decisive phase of the war in the Mediterranean has begun. Nationalist military circles in Iraq see in this the confirmation that the *coup d'état* carried out by the army has occurred at the right moment, not only from the point of view of the country's interest, but also in relation to the overall situation. . . . There is a widespread conviction that Axis forces will soon put in an appearance in this area, either from the north or from the south, and that the inevitable decisive battle of the Mediterranean theatre will be fought in Mesopotamia.[8]

Unfortunately for the Iraqis, this was wishful thinking. Since the Italian defeats in the Balkans and North

[8] *G.F.M.*, 792, 27298.

Africa at the end of 1940, Mussolini was almost totally dependent upon Germany to keep his forces in the field, and although, as we shall see, he occasionally appeared to display a real interest in exploiting developments in Iraq, he was powerless to act decisively on his own. In Germany, the Foreign Ministry under von Ribbentrop also seems to have realized the possibilities inherent in the Iraqi situation, but it is clear that Hitler, although goaded into taking some action, regarded Iraq as a side-show which must not be allowed to divert attention away from the imminent invasion of the Soviet Union.

On 9 April Woermann briefed von Ribbentrop on the situation in Iraq at the latter's request, explaining that 'there was now . . . a cabinet which was to be considered the most nationalist and pro-Axis thus far, and that according to available reports this cabinet had the full support of the Iraq army.' It 'was putting up stiff resistance to the English wishes for the stationing of English troops in Iraq and a more or less unrestricted right of passage.' Regarding material support, Woermann said that discussions with the Japanese concerning arms deliveries had still not resulted in a positive outcome and that Afghanistan had now been approached with a view to sending 'camouflaged arms shipments . . . by a special route'. There was still, however, the problem of what could be delivered, as Hitler had yet to make a decision on this matter. Von Ribbentrop promptly authorized Woermann, 'subject to fundamental policy decisions, to proceed . . . with the handling of this problem and all others connected with it and to push them vigorously. In so far as a decision by the Fuehrer was necessary, he [von Ribbentrop] would obtain it.' The foreign minister emphasized that 'in case no decision against England was obtained this year, the questions of the Middle East might become of decisive importance perhaps beginning with this autumn, and he instructed [Woermann] to take particular care of these questions . . .' He also authorized the *Abwehr*'s earlier proposal to carry out sabotage in

Palestine, Transjordan and Iraq, providing he was kept informed of the individual projects.[9]

During the course of the same day, Woermann received an Italian proposal for a joint Axis statement to be given to Rashid 'Ali. The Italians believed that hostilities between Iraq and Britain were likely to break out in the near future and that the former could not hold out for long without Axis support. In view of the geographical difficulties of providing this support, the Italians advocated a cautious statement in the following terms:

> (1) That [Rashid 'Ali's] action is being followed by Italy and Germany with sympathy; (2) That in view of the difficulty so far of finding a way in which to supply Iraq with arms and ammunition, it would appear expedient to delay an armed conflict; (3) That in the event such a conflict proved unavoidable, the Axis powers would give Iraq every possible support and would also supply her with war material as soon as a route for its transit could be found.

Woermann regarded this draft as 'too weak' and produced one of his own in which the Iraqi prime minister was to be told:

> (1) That Italy and Germany follow his actions with the greatest sympathy; (2) That Italy and Germany advise armed resistance against England as soon as the relationship of the forces involved offers promise of success; (3) That Italy and Germany even at this time are actively preparing assistance in the form of arms and ammunition and hope to overcome the well-known difficulties with respect to the transport route. . . . The Italian and German governments are also prepared to give the Iraq government financial support and would like to be informed of its present wishes in this respect.

The Italians accepted the German counterdraft and Gabbrielli reported that it created a good impression with the Iraqi government.[10]

[9] *D.G.F.P.*, Vol. XII, No. 299.
[10] *G.F.M.*, 83, 61561; *D.G.F.P.*, Vol. XII, No. 322.

Although his foreign ministry had proposed only
lukewarm encouragement to Rashid 'Ali, Mussolini, inspired by the Axis advance in the Balkans and North
Africa, revived the idea of a vast pincer movement
against Egypt in a conversation with the German military
attaché in Rome on 13 April. The attache reported that:

> The Duce took this opportunity to emphasize the mortal
> effect upon the British Empire if the Italo-German advance
> [in North Africa] could be continued to the Suez Canal
> and if the British position in the Middle East could also
> be attacked from the east with the help or benevolent
> neutrality of Turkey. The possession of this centre of the
> British Empire with its oil wells might have an even more
> profound effect upon the British world position than a
> landing in the British Isles themselves.[11]

Hitler, however, threw cold water on any suggestion
of an advance through Turkey when he met Ciano a
week later at Muenchenkirchen. He declared that:

> The possibility of attempting the operation by force can
> be ruled out. Independently of Turkish resistance, which
> would be considerable, the distance would make any mili-
> tary operation uncertain and dangerous. Diplomatically,
> too, it seems difficult to draw Turkey into the orbit of
> the Axis, at least within a short space of time. Difficult
> because there are certain active cliques, which are very
> hostile to the Axis . . .; difficult, too, because it is im-
> possible to see what political advantages could be offered
> to Turkey in exchange.[12]

These, of course, were not the real reasons for Hitler's
reluctance. His eyes were riveted upon the forthcoming
campaign against the Soviet Union and the operations in
the Balkans were intended to secure his southern flank
for that and not as a preliminary to an invasion of the
Middle East through Turkey. Incredible though it may
seem, however, the Fuehrer had not given his Italian

[11] Unpublished report of the German military attaché in Rome
deposited at the Imperial War Museum in London.
[12] Malcolm Muggeridge (Ed.) *Ciano's Diplomatic Papers*, London,
Odhams, 1948, p. 435.

allies the slightest inkling of his plans in this respect.

In the meantime, the British had informed Rashid 'Ali of the imminent arrival of the first detachment of Indian troops at Basra. On 18 April the prime minister told Gabbrielli that:

> The National Council for the Defence of Iraq had met yesterday morning and studied the situation. On the basis of [its] decision . . . he [announced] . . . the following: the Iraq government was firmly resolved to defend itself and would therefore like to learn as soon as possible from the Axis governments: first, whether the Iraq army could count on support from the air force of the Axis powers; the air- fields of Iraq would of course be placed at the disposal of the Axis powers. Second, whether the Iraq army could count on receiving rifles and ammunition by air trans- ports. . . . In any case he . . . requested that all the help which the Iraq government had requested even earlier be made available to it and that financial aid also be given.[13]

There were two important novelties about this request. In the first place, the Iraqis were, for the first time, asking not just for Axis arms, but for direct Axis inter- vention. Secondly, there was no mention of political declarations or any of the other paraphernalia associated with earlier Iraqi requests for Axis support. Things had become too urgent for that.

Relaying this information to the German embassy in Rome, Ciano's head of cabinet said that while 'the Duce was in principle prepared to grant the Iraq government the aid requested . . . the possibility of doing so seemed to him extremely limited.' The Italian military authori- ties would examine the question in more detail, but 'it would probably be easier for Germany to render military assistance . . .'[14]

Von Ribbentrop had obtained Hitler's consent for the despatch of arms to Iraq on 10 April but, as he pointed out in a memorandum to the Fuehrer on 21 April, 'speedy assistance is possible only by air', and this the

[13] *D.G.F.P.*, Vol. XII, No. 372.
[14] Idem.

Iraqis had now requested. 'Direct intervention by *Luftwaffe* units in Iraq is out of the question,' the foreign minister continued, 'since that exceeds the range of the *Luftwaffe*.' It appeared possible to fly arms to Iraq in individual aircraft, provided they could stop over in Syria, which would require clearance from the Vichy authorities. As British troops had now landed at Basra, moreover, there was some doubt about Iraq's staying power, but he requested 'a decision . . . as to whether arms deliveries to Iraq by plane are to be started, if it appears that the Iraq government still has the will to resist.'[15]

Hitler was at first inclined to reject his foreign minister's proposal. An erroneous report from army intelligence suggested that there were already 14,000 Indian troops in Iraq with another 14,000 on the way and that, as a result, any German assistance would be too late. It is also interesting to note that on the very day von Ribbentrop put forward his proposal, Hitler decided to launch a massive airborne invasion of Crete. It apparently never occurred to him that he might use his airborne troops in Iraq instead, although it is recorded that Churchill believed that he 'cast away the opportunity of taking a great prize for little cost in the Middle East' by not doing so.[16]

Meanwhile, the Iraqis were becoming irritated by the lack of action on the part of the Axis. Following a meeting with Rashid 'Ali and the Mufti on 24 April, Gabbrielli reported that 'the [Iraq] government is quite annoyed because it has as yet received no reply to its request for support by Axis aviation . . . while the situation, which is already extremely delicate, could in three or four days become downright critical. The annoyance is all the greater since [Haddad] brought back with him from Berlin the most optimistic impression about the possibility of obtaining such aid.' Rashid 'Ali appealed for the despatch of a high-ranking Italian

[15] Ibid., No. 377.
[16] Churchill, *Second World War*, Vol. III, p. 236.

officer from the armistice commission in Syria to draw up plans for joint action, and urged an intensification of Arabic language propaganda, in favour of Iraq, by Berlin and Bari radios.[17]

Once again von Ribbentrop took the matter to the Fuehrer. Although he deprecated the exaggerated estimates of the number of British troops in Iraq, he skilfully played upon Hitler's desire to have a friendly Turkey at the time of Germany's attack upon Russia, by suggesting that if the British did establish themselves in strength in Iraq, they would use their position to prepare a move into Syria and to put pressure on the Turks. Outlining the various possibilities for sending arms and ammunition to Iraq, he said that the French would be approached to release *matériel* stored in Syria, and that air supply by the *Luftwaffe* 'could be prepared to the point where it would require only an order at the proper moment'. Regarding more active intervention, the foreign minister said that air support for the Iraqi army 'has been discussed with the *Luftwaffe* Operations Staff in a preparatory and informational manner', but that 'whether further military commitment by the Axis will be possible in the future, perhaps by way of Syria, depends on the further development of German-French relations.' Before making any final decision it was still necessary to obtain more information about the situation and 'the Iraq government should by no means be induced to enter into an open fight against England until it is certain that Iraq is strong enough with the aid of the Axis to hold her own against the English.'[18]

But as we saw earlier, time was running out for Rashid 'Ali. On 28 April Cornwallis told him of the imminent arrival of the second detachment of Indian troops at Basra and on 2 May hostilities broke out at Habbaniya. The Iraqi minister in Ankara, who happened to be Rashid 'Ali's brother, informed the German embassy of the outbreak of fighting. 'Relations with England have

[17] *D.G.F.P.*, Vol. XII, No. 401.
[18] Ibid., No. 415.

been broken off', ran the embassy's report of his *démarche*.

> The Iraq government requests that Minister Grobba be sent to Baghdad at once so that diplomatic relations may be resumed. It also requests immediate military aid. In particular a considerable number of airplanes in order to prevent further English landings and to drive the English from the airfields. The English have a total of 8,500 troops on Iraq territory, including the recently landed forces, and the Iraqi have 50,000 men under arms. They want to raise another 50,000 and weapons for them are urgently needed. The Iraq minister asked for an answer by tomorrow if in any way possible.[19]

The time for procrastination was clearly past. The Germans had to make up their minds whether or not to go to the aid of Iraq. In a memorandum for Hitler on 3 May von Ribbentrop supported the proposal to send Grobba to Baghdad and suggested that he be accompanied by liaison officers from the army and the *Luftwaffe*. The latter would have to assess whether facilities were adequate to accommodate German aircraft, but it was up to the Fuehrer to decide whether he wanted preparations for air shipment of *matériel* to go ahead. 'Would it not be the best help,' von Ribbentrop asked, 'to transfer a fighter and a bomber squadron [to Iraq] immediately if the question of landing should be clarified in a positive sense . . . ?' Supporting positive action, the foreign minister argued:

> If the available reports are correct regarding the relatively small forces the English have landed in Iraq so far, there would seem to be a great opportunity for establishing a base for warfare against England through an armed Iraq. A constantly expanding insurrection of the Arab world would be of the greatest help in the preparation of our decisive advance toward Egypt.[20]

[19] *D.G.F.P.*, Vol. XII, No. 432.
[20] Ibid., No. 435.

After a careful study of von Ribbentrop's memorandum, the appeal from Rashid 'Ali's brother and a detailed tabulation of the Iraqi general staff's immediate requirements in arms and ammunition (which had been forwarded by the Italians), Hitler expressed complete agreement with the foreign minister's proposals and voiced the desire 'that everything possible be done with regard to military support'. He was sceptical about the possibility of using the *Luftwaffe*, but 'finally said that if it should prove to be true [as the Iraqis had claimed] that there were sufficient supplies of fuel in Iraq, the planes would then have the possibility of making return flights and thus might be able to take over certain transports.' The one problem was that the Iraqi army, which was accustomed to using British equipment, asked for such items as .50-in anti-tank rifles and Vickers .303-in machine-guns. 'The calibres for ammunition, etc., cited in the list of things wanted were entirely unknown to him', the perplexed Fuehrer confessed; 'we did not have these.'[21]

If Hitler had taken these decisions a month or even a fortnight earlier, they might have made a considerable difference to the prospects for Iraqi resistance. But by delaying them until fighting had actually begun and more Indian troops had landed at Basra, he laid himself open to the charge of sending 'too little, too late'. Certainly Rashid 'Ali's forces crumpled before they could properly benefit from what help the Axis powers were able to send them.

Although it was technically possible for the more long-range German and Italian aircraft to fly directly to Iraq from bases in Greece or the Dodecanese, it was obviously desirable that they should be able to stop over somewhere *en route*. Such facilities would also enable shorter range aircraft, especially fighters, to make the journey. Not only was Syria the obvious choice as a staging post, but, as von Ribbentrop had pointed out in

[21] *D.G.F.P.*, Vol. XII, No. 436.

one of his memoranda to Hitler, some of the war *matériel* stocked there could be sent to the Iraqis by an overland route. Vichy therefore became a key element in the German plan to assist Iraq.

It was fortunate for the Germans that the Vichy government was only too anxious to oblige. The earlier plans for French participation in Hitler's 'continental coalition' against Britain had fizzled out by the end of 1940, not only because the Fuehrer, increasingly dominated by the desire to settle accounts with the Soviet Union, had gradually lost interest in them, but also because the dismissal of Marshal Pétain's pro-German deputy, Pierre Laval, on 13 December, 1940, although carried out for domestic reasons, had destroyed what little faith the German leader had had in French reliability. Relations between Germany and Vichy had been extremely cool ever since. Laval's successor, Admiral François Darlan, was desperately seeking to convince the Germans of his goodwill, in order to improve France's treatment under the armistice agreement and her prospects in the post-war world which he thought would emerge from the inevitable German victory.

The German desire to make use of Syria provided just such an opportunity. On 8 May it was reported to Berlin that French representatives had agreed to the following concessions:

(a) The stocks of French arms under Italian control in Syria to be made available for arms transports to Iraq; (b) Assistance in the forwarding of arms shipments of other origin that arrive in Syria by land or sea for Iraq; (c) Permission for German planes, destined for Iraq, to make intermediate landings and to take on gasoline in Syria; (d) Cession to Iraq of reconnaissance, pursuit, and bombing planes, as well as bombs, from the air force permitted for Syria under the armistice treaty; (e) An airfield in Syria to be made available especially for the intermediate landing of German planes; (f) Until such an airfield has been made available, an order to be issued to all airfields in Syria to assist German planes making intermediate landings.

It was emphasized that 'these . . . concessions go considerably beyond what could have been expected on the German side.'[22]

It is an interesting reflection upon the nature of the Axis alliance that when the question of landing rights in Syria was first broached, the Germans told the French not to tell the Italians anything about it! This was a game which the French, who had always deeply resented Italy's masquerade as the joint victor in the 1940 campaign, were only too happy to play. Similarly, when the Italians asked for stop-over facilities in Syria for their own aircraft on 7 May, they did not bother to inform the Germans. The latter were told of the Italian request by the French government, which was said to be 'very averse to complying with [it] . . . because it finds the appearance of the Italian air force in Syria undesirable.' As a result the Italians 'narrowed down their demand explaining that this was for the time being only a general inquiry and that there was no question as yet of actually sending planes.' Commenting on this information, Woermann wrote: 'It would seem to me that the German operations by way of Syria would actually be endangered by simultaneous Italian action in that area. Desirable as simultaneous Italian effort is, it ought to be suggested that it would be better concentrated elsewhere.'[23] This uncomradely advice was not accepted, however, and the Germans seem to have ended up by putting pressure upon the French to grant the Italians the same stop-over facilities as had been conceded to them.

The bizarre flight of Rudolf Hess to Scotland on the night of 10/11 May prompted von Ribbentrop to make a sudden visit to Rome on the 13th and 14th to explain away the action of the Fuehrer's erstwhile deputy. While in the Italian capital he also took the opportunity of

[22] *D.G.F.P.*, Vol. XII, No. 475.
[23] Ibid., No. 479.

discussing the situation in Syria and Iraq, and in what appears to be the only explicit German reference to the possibility, stated that 'if a sizable arms shipment reached Iraq, airborne troops could then be brought into the area, which could then with the material on hand advance against the English and from Iraq, in certain circumstances, they could attack Egypt from the east.' The German foreign minister may simply have been pandering to Mussolini's known interest in such an operation, or, as someone who was not entirely convinced of the wisdom of invading the Soviet Union, he may have been floating a trial balloon of his own. Whatever the reason, the Duce was enthusiastic '. . . Iraq had to be helped in any case,' he said, 'for in this way a new front would be opened up against the English and a revolt not only of the Arabs, but also of a great number of Mohammedans would be started.'[24] Outlining Italy's own plans for sending arms and aircraft to Iraq, he suggested that 'should the shipment of arms through Turkey be impossible, one would have to march against England from Syria.' This would be much easier than advancing from Libya, for the Axis armies would only have to cross 100 kilometres of desert instead of 500. In reply to a question from von Ribbentrop, Mussolini said that Rashid 'Ali 'had stated that he could hold his own against the English if he could only get some war material. If he got no help, however, then . . . resistance would be broken . . . in three to four weeks.'[25]

In the meantime, German support for Iraq was on its way. The newly appointed diplomatic representative, Fritz Grobba, arrived in Mosul on 10 May with two Heinkel He 111 bombers. Two days later, his *Luftwaffe* liaison officer, Major Axel von Blomberg, flew to Baghdad in another He 111. He had the misfortune to

[24] It is interesting to note that the Chief of the Imperial General Staff wrote to General Auchinleck on 21 May: 'The Arab world as such does not worry me but the Muslim world as a whole does – very much.' See Connell, *Auchinleck*, p 237.
[25] *D.G.F.P.*, Vol. XII, No. 511.

arrive over the Iraqi capital in the middle of a dogfight between British and Iraqi fighters, and was shot dead by a stray British bullet.[26] After his death, a Colonel Jungk was appointed *Luftwaffe* commander in Iraq and he brought a squadron of He 111's and one of Messerschmitt Me 110 twin-engined fighter-bombers to Mosul on 15 May, a total of twenty-four aircraft. They were in action on the following day. In order to disguise their origin, the German planes had been specially painted with Iraqi insignia. Meanwhile, a special foreign ministry envoy, Rudolf Rahn (the French had indicated that they did not want the return of von Hentig), had arrived in Syria on 9 May to organize the supply of *matériel*. This was to be despatched by rail from Aleppo, but the Turks, through whose territory part of the line ran, insisted on five days' notice being given for each shipment. In an effort to get around this delay, Rahn suggested to General Dentz that he tell the Turks that the *matériel* was not destined for Iraq, but to reinforce Vichy's own border garrisons. The High Commissioner followed this suggestion and Turkish agreement was obtained in a matter of hours. The first trainload of French war *matériel* arrived in Mosul on 13 May, only seventy-five hours after Rahn's first meeting with Dentz. The Turks were annoyed when they found out that they had been deceived, but surprisingly did not place any obstacle in the way of further shipments.

The first British reaction to the outbreak of hostilities in Iraq was to restore operational control over the country to Middle East Command, and to urge Wavell to secure the Basra-Habbaniya lines of communication, if possible by inciting the Euphrates tribes to rebel against Rashid 'Ali. The Commander-in-Chief was not at all pleased by these additional responsibilities. In a cable to the Chiefs-of-Staff on 3 May he said:

[26] Most accounts state that Blomberg was killed by Iraqi anti-aircraft fire. But Grobba, who was present at the airfield when his plane landed, is positive that the bullet came from a British aircraft.

I have consistently warned you that no assistance could be given to Iraq from Palestine in present circumstances and have always advised that commitment in Iraq should be avoided . . . My forces are stretched to limit everywhere and I simply cannot afford to risk part of forces on what cannot produce any effect. I do not see how I can possibly accept military responsibility for force at Basra . . . and consider this must be controlled from India. I can only advise negotiation with Iraqis on basis of liquidation of regrettable incident by mutual agreement with alternative of war with British Empire, complete blockade and ruthless air action.[27]

Later on the same day he offered to scrape together a small force from Palestine, but warned that it would leave that country, where there was a danger of rebellion, in an extremely weak position. He also felt that it would not serve any useful purpose in Iraq and once again advised a negotiated settlement.

Mediation had in fact been proposed by the Turkish government. Its motives are easy enough to understand. Treading a very delicate path between conflicting pressures from Germany and Britain, it had no wish to see Iraq either occupied by the former or blockaded by the latter. The British government, however, was not interested. It took the view that Rashid 'Ali must be got rid of and that since the arrival of Indian troops at Basra had forced him to show his hand before the Axis powers had had time to come to his aid, there was a good chance of doing so provided quick action was taken. The British ambassador in Ankara was therefore instructed to inform the Turks that their intervention would only be of value in persuading Rashid 'Ali to withdraw his forces unconditionally from Habbaniya, and that they would be better employed in trying to obtain the replacement of the prime minister and his supporters by a more friendly government. But the Turkish government was not prepared to act on either of these suggestions.

There is conflicting evidence concerning Iraqi wil-

[27] Connell, *Wavell*, p. 435.

lingness to accept the Turkish offer of mediation. On 8 May the Iraqi government sent Naji Shawkat, who was defence minister in Rashid 'Ali's cabinet, to Ankara for conversations with the Turks. Rashid 'Ali told Grobba on the 12th that Turkey had proposed 'orally and in writing' mediation on the following terms: '1. Cessation of Iraq military operations and withdrawal of Iraq troops. 2. Permission to establish English military bases in the country for the protection of troops in transit to Transjordan. 3. Recognition of Rashid 'Ali's government.'[28] The Iraqi prime minister feared that these proposals presaged Turkish military intervention in Iraq, a fear which the Germans quite rightly discounted. Naji Shawkat, on the other hand, told von Papen on the 13th that his government had accepted Turkish mediation, but only in order to gain time, 'for he was firmly convinced that an agreement on the proposed basis – return to the *status quo ante* – would not come about. England had to eliminate the Gaylani government and seize the places in the country that were of military importance. He therefore considered the outcome of the mediation action pessimistically.'[29]

Further confusion is created by Shawkat's, and other Iraqis', post-war testimony to the effect that he advised the government to accept the Turkish proposals and that Rashid 'Ali, after consulting his ministers, was prepared to do so. However, the 'Golden Square' objected and Colonel Sabbagh actually threatened to shoot the prime minister if he temporized. Rashid 'Ali in turn threatened to resign, and the breach was only healed by the Mufti, who reminded the government of their duty to carry out the Arab mission. According to these accounts, the 'Golden Square' were confident of Axis support and Sabbagh assured the cabinet that the Iraqi army could hold out for over three months, if necessary, until it arrived.

The optimism of the 'Golden Square' was matched only by the pessimism of General Wavell. Replying to

[28] *D.G.F.P.*, Vol. XII, No. 503.
[29] Ibid., No. 514.

the Chiefs-of-Staff's re-affirmation of the need to intervene and their refusal to consider the Turkish offer of
mediation, he cabled bluntly on 5 May: 'You must face
facts.' The force being gathered on the frontier between
Transjordan and Iraq (which was codenamed HAB-
FORCE) could not be ready before 10 May at the
earliest and could not reach Habbaniya before the 12th,
assuming that there was no Iraqi resistance. Expressing
his doubts as to whether the force was strong enough to
relieve the beleaguered garrison, or even whether the
latter could hold out until it arrived, he warned 'in
gravest possible terms' that he felt that the 'prolongation
of fighting in Iraq will seriously endanger defence of
Palestine and Egypt. Apart from the weakening of
strength by detachments such as above, political repercussions will be incalculable and may result in what I
have spent nearly two years trying to avoid, serious
internal trouble in our bases. I therefore urge again most
strongly that settlement should be negotiated as early
as possible.'[30]

Churchill's reaction to Wavell's renewed plea for
negotiation was little short of contemptuous. 'Why should
the force mentioned, which seems considerable, be
deemed insufficient to deal with the Iraq army?' he
asked General Ismay of the Chiefs-of-Staff committee on
6 May.

> . . . Why should the troops at Habbaniya give in before
> 12 May? Their losses have been nominal as so far reported
> . . . How can a settlement be negotiated, as General Wavell
> suggests? Suppose the Iraqis, under German instigation,
> insist upon our evacuating Basra, or moving in small
> detachments at their mercy across the country to Palestine.
> The opinion of the senior naval officer at Basra is that a
> collapse or surrender there would be disastrous. This is
> also the opinion of the government of India. I am deeply
> disturbed at General Wavell's attitude. He seems to have
> been taken as much by surprise on his eastern as he was on

[30] Connell, *Wavell*, pp 437-38.

his western [i.e. Libyan] flank . . . He gives me the impression of being tired out.[31]

The prime minister was being a little hard on his local commander, who was facing continuous and heavy demands for action on all sides, but there can be little doubt that this instinct in favour of striking a quick blow in Iraq was right. As if to demonstrate the wisdom of his approach, the garrison at Habbaniya forced the Iraqis to raise the siege on the very day that the minute to Ismay was written, although they remained cut off from outside support.

Indian interest in Iraq, and greater willingness to shoulder burdens there, was underlined on 9 May by a message from General Auchinleck to the Chief of the Imperial General Staff, General Sir John Dill. 'In our opinion', Auchinleck wrote, 'there is now only one policy which will call a definite halt to German penetration into Iraq, Iran and possibly Turkey and Syria . . . This policy is to establish ourselves with the minimum delay in sufficient force at Baghdad and other key points such as Mosul and Kirkuk so as to be able to resist any attack internal or external by the Axis.'[32] These views were supported in a telegram from the Viceroy to the India Office on the following day.

From Wavell's standpoint, it was bad enough to be asked to relieve Habbaniya and, as Churchill had urged, to go on from there to Baghdad. Now he was being advised to take Kirkuk and Mosul as well. Commenting on Auchinleck's proposal, he wrote: 'At this critical period essential that our limited resources be concentrated on our really vital military interests. In Iraq these are . . . as follows: (a) Avoidance of major conflict with Arabs. (b) Security of oil supplies from Abadan. (c) Security of oil supplies from Iraq. (d) Maintenance of air route to India.' All these, however, were 'of minor importance' when set against the security of Egypt and Palestine.

[31] Churchill, *Second World War*, Vol. III, pp 228-29.
[32] Connell, *Auchinleck*, p. 221.

India, Wavell argued, did not fully appreciate the
effect which a large-scale Arab uprising could have upon
the military situation in the Middle East. 'It would
have repercussions in Palestine, Aden, Yemen, Egypt
and Syria which might absorb very large proportion of
my force in maintaining internal order . . . Unless
we can get back to normal relations with well-disposed
Iraqi government at very early date suggestions that we
propose to occupy country and suppress Iraqi independence will be exploited by enemy with serious results.'
As far as oil supplies were concerned, those from Iraq
were subject to Iraqi goodwill and could not be secured
by military force, while the Abadan refineries could only
be protected by a force in Basra and the maintenance of
the outlet to the Persian Gulf. The air route to India
could be kept open as long as Habbaniya and Basra remained in British hands. There was therefore no need
to occupy Mosul or Kirkuk, which was not within British
resources anyway. Wavell did not believe that there was
any danger of the Germans advancing on these towns,
especially in the light of evidence of increasing tension
between Germany and the Soviet Union. If German
forces did secure passage through Turkey, he felt that
they would be much more likely to advance through
Syria in the direction of Palestine and Egypt than to
make for northern Iraq.

Indeed, Wavell was not even in favour of occupying
Baghdad, except as a temporary measure to establish a
favourable Iraqi government, or at the latter's request.
He proposed:

(a) To do everything possible to secure political settlement
. . . as soon as possible and to resume normal relations with
Iraqi government. (b) Force at Basra to secure and organize base and endeavour to establish good relations with tribes
but not to move forward till strong enough to be effective
which I do not feel will be for some little time. (c)
HABFORCE will move from Palestine to Habbaniya and

thence if situation permits to Baghdad with view to influencing political situation.[33]

In an obvious attempt to reassure Wavell, Churchill cabled him in the small hours of 13 May: 'You do not need to bother too much about the long future in Iraq. Your immediate task is to get a friendly government set up in Baghdad, and to beat down Rashid 'Ali's forces with the utmost vigour. We do not wish to be involved at present in any large-scale advance up the river from Basra, nor have we prescribed the occupation of Kirkuk or Mosul. We do not seek any change in the independent status of Iraq, and full instructions have been given in accordance with your own ideas on this point.' However, the prime minister emphasized, 'what matters is action; namely, the swift advance of the mobile column to establish effective contact between Baghdad and Palestine. Every day counts, for the Germans may not be long.'[34] This final warning was given added seriousness by the news, first received on 12 May, of the arrival of German aircraft in Syria.

Later on 13 May HABFORCE, which had been assembled at H4, a pumping station on the oil pipeline from Kirkuk to Haifa,[35] crossed the Transjordanian frontier into Iraq. Part of this force consisted of Arab troops, units of the Transjordan Frontier Force and the Arab Legion. It was natural for the Amir 'Abdullah to offer his forces, which were in any case British-trained, British-officered and British-equipped, to help restore his relatives to power, but there were some doubts about their reliability. 'Will the Arab Legion fight?' General Wilson, who had just taken over command in Palestine, asked Major Glubb. 'The Arab Legion will fight anybody', was Glubb's reply and his confidence was entirely

[33] Connell, *Auchinleck*, pp 222-23.
[34] Churchill, *Second World War*, Vol. III, p. 231.
[35] As indicated earlier (see above, p. 23), the Iraq oil pipeline had two branches, one to Haifa in Palestine and the other to Tripoli in the Lebanon. The pumping stations on these branches were designated with the letters H and T respectively and were numbered in ascending order as one travelled westwards. See Map.

justified, although a squadron of the Transjordan Frontier Force did mutiny, claiming 'that there is no quarrel
with the Iraqis and that the British made others fight
for them.'[86]

Although HABFORCE was attacked by some of the
German aircraft which had by now arrived in Iraq, it
did not meet with much resistance from the Iraqi army
and an advance column reached Habbaniya, which was
some 300 miles across the desert, on 18 May. The Arab
Legion cut the Baghdad-Mosul railway to the north of
the Iraqi capital, upon which the British forces prepared
to march.

It was precisely as Iraqi resistance was crumbling that
Hitler issued his Military Directive No. 30 on the
Middle East. 'The *Arab liberation movement* in the
Middle East is our natural ally against England', it proclaimed. 'In this connection the rising in Iraq has special
importance. It strengthens beyond the boundaries of
Iraq the forces hostile to England in the Middle East,
disturbs English communications, and ties down English
troops and shipping space at the expense of other
theatres of war.' The Fuehrer had 'therefore decided to
advance developments in the Middle East by giving
assistance to Iraq', including 'the dispatch of a military
mission . . . (cover name: Special Staff F) . . . under
General of the *Luftwaffe* Felmy.'

The main fault with this directive was that it came
several weeks too late, and even now Hitler showed signs
of downgrading its importance by making it clear that
'whether and how the English position between the
Mediterranean and the Persian Gulf – in connection with
an offensive against the Suez Canal – shall later be
definitively defeated, is to be decided only after BAR-
BAROSSA.' Nor was there much prospect of any more
short-term assistance in the air, where it was most
needed. The *Luftwaffe* was now heavily committed in
the assault upon Crete, which had begun on 20 May,

[86] Glubb, *Arab Legion*, p. 257; Wilson, *Eight Years*, p. 106.

and the Fuehrer directive specifically stated that its use in Iraq was 'to be limited in numbers.'[37]

On the Iraqi side, the realities of the situation were at last beginning to sink in. On 24 May the Mufti told Gabrielli that in spite of the good prospects for a revolt in the rest of the Arab world, 'all this is only of limited value if the current uprising in Iraq, which in his opinion is the key to the situation, should fail.' What worried him most 'was not so much the general military situation as the political situation at the moment. There was no lack of timorous pessimists . . . who were endeavouring both covertly and in the open to sabotage the efforts of the Mufti and Gaylani, who was fighting like a lion. Even the cabinet included some individuals who held that if the Axis powers did not render immediate and substantial assistance, it might be better to negotiate with the English.'[38] The Mufti believed that 'the next fourteen days would be of decisive importance. If they were unable to last through this period, it would be necessary to give in.' Arguing that 'the aircraft that had arrived to date were insufficient in number', the Mufti appealed for more, and for war *matériel,* 'as proof of tangible solidarity', warning that 'if Iraq should fall during these coming days, the anti-English movement throughout the whole Middle East would step by step succumb to British arms or to British gold and intrigues.' The Axis was admittedly equipped to cope with this situation, but if it occurred, 'it would be necessary . . . to reconquer one position after another by force of arms, without being able to rely on the present militant spirit and the aid of the Arab world, which was now still at its disposal.'[39]

This conversation seems to have had a considerable effect upon Mussolini. When he saw the German military

[37] *D.G.F.P.,* Vol. XII, No. 543.
[38] This may be an allusion to Naji Shawkat, who, by his own account, advocated an understanding with Britain on his return from Turkey, only to be denounced as a traitor by the 'Golden Square'.
[39] *D.G.F.P.,* Vol. XII, No. 557.

attaché on 26 May, he observed that while the situation in Iraq was not clear, it seemed impossible that the present position could be maintained for long. 'Do we want to furnish effective or only symbolic assistance?' he asked. He favoured the former because an opportunity thereby existed to bring about a revolt of 'all the peoples of the east' against Britain. But they would lose heart if Iraq collapsed. If Germany shared his views, the Duce argued, it would be necessary to occupy Cyprus – 'the key to the entire Orient' – after Crete was taken. 'Once we are sitting in Crete and Cyprus,' he declared, 'the position of the British fleet in the eastern Mediterranean will be so threatened by air power that it will scarcely be able to remain even in Alexandria.' Nevertheless, he concluded, if an examination of the situation showed that it was impossible to give Rashid 'Ali prompt and energetic assistance, it would be better to tell him so.[40]

In reply, the military attaché was instructed to tell the Italian leader that

> energetic assistance, and not a gesture, is also the German intention. The first success is the delivery of three-quarters of the French war *matériel* stocked in Syria to Iraq. The opening of the supply route through Turkey is being striven for. Transit of oil and petrol is already agreed. Every possible supply of arms and aircraft by Italy is urgently desired. Cyprus cannot be taken by a German airborne action as the distance, even from Rhodes, is too great to protect troop carriers with fighters. Nevertheless, everything will be attempted to convey help to Iraq, partly by sea and partly by air.[41]

Despite the arrival as late as 27 May of the first squadron of Italian CR 42 fighters, however, there was now little that could be done to save the situation in Iraq. Rashid 'Ali took it all rather badly. After a conversation

[40] Unpublished report of the German military attaché in Rome deposited at the Imperial War Museum, London.
[41] Unpublished OKW directive deposited at the Ministry of Defence for the Navy, London.

with him that same evening, Gabbrielli reported that he
'seemed to me to be more embittered than anxious. In
his own words, German help has been rapid but meagre
and he is beginning to fear that Iraq is being regarded as
a pawn by Germany, who does not wish to commit herself wholeheartedly. He also told me that he had expected more from Italy.'[42] Two days later, false information,
deliberately spread by the British, to the effect that there
were tanks in their column advancing on Baghdad led
the German minister to leave the capital for Kirkuk.
Rashid 'Ali appealed for *Luftwaffe* support to defend
Baghdad, but maintained that even if he lost the city, he
intended 'to continue defending the country and to retreat step by step.'[43] This was soon exposed as so much
bombast, however, for on the following day, when
Grobba moved to Mosul, the Iraqi prime minister, together with Gabbrielli, the Mufti and other prominent
rebels, fled across the border into Iran.

From Mosul Grobba reported on 30 May that the
local army commanders were 'determined to continue the
fight if Germany immediately promises effective military
aid.'[44] Von Ribbentrop replied that more aircraft were
on their way and would probably arrive in Mosul on 1
June, only to be told by Grobba that they could not land,
either there or at Kirkuk, because of the danger and the
shortage of aviation spirit, and that they would have to
operate from Syrian bases. Later the same day, 31 May,
Grobba reported that an armistice had been signed in
Baghdad, and in response to another false rumour that
the British had captured Mosul airfield, he promptly left
for Syria. Late that night, Field-Marshal Keitel, the
head of the OKW, cabled General Felmy, who had not
had time even to get to Iraq, that 'all German forces
are to gather at Alep[po]. There complete reserve is
to be exercised until further intentions have been
clarified with the French government in Vichy. Re-

[42] *G.F.M.*, 83, 61900-02.
[43] *D.G.F.P.*, Vol. XII, No. 568.
[44] *D.G.F.P.*, Vol. XII, No. 571.

move Iraq insignia. Further orders will follow.'[45]

In Baghdad, the mayor and army officers who had not pulled out with the rebels approached the British embassy, which had been blockaded since the outbreak of hostilities, on 30 May with the request to arrange an armistice. This was signed on the 31st and was followed on 1 June by the return of 'Abd al-Ilah to the Iraqi capital. The British triumph was, however, marred by riots in the Jewish quarter of Baghdad on 2 and 3 June, in which over 150 Jews were killed, hundreds injured and many houses and shops looted. The most disgraceful aspect of this unsavoury episode, which appears to have been the handiwork of supporters of Rashid 'Ali, is that the British troops, who could easily have restored order, were not permitted to enter the city. According to one of their officers, this was the result of instructions from the Foreign Office in London. 'From the hour of the cease fire their word had prevailed', he wrote. 'Having fought our way, step by step, to the threshold of the city, we must now cool our heels outside. It would, apparently, be lowering to the dignity of our ally, the Regent, if he were seen to be supported on arrival by British bayonets.'[46]

A new government under Jamil al-Midfa'i was announced on 4 June. On the 9th it symbolically demonstrated its good faith by breaking off diplomatic relations with Italy.

After a decent interval, Nuri as-Sa'id returned to power in October 1941, and his régime was marked by tough measures against the supporters of Rashid 'Ali. Three members of the 'Golden Square' were captured by the British when they and the Russians occupied Iran in August 1941. Two were handed over to the Iraqi government in 1942 and the remaining one in 1944. All were tried and hanged. The leader, Colonel Salah ad-Din as-Sabbagh, managed to elude capture in Iran and eventu-

[45] Ibid., No. 577.
[46] Somerset de Chair, *The Golden Carpet*, London, Faber & Faber, 1944, p. 118.

ally escaped into Turkey. But he was handed over by the Turkish authorities in 1945 and he too was tried and hanged. Rashid 'Ali and the Mufti also escaped to Turkey, but they went on to Germany and more intrigues. After the war they managed to avoid the fate of their military backers.

On 2 June 1941 Field Marshal Keitel gave his Italian opposite number, General Cavallero, the following summary of the reasons for the collapse of the Iraqi revolt:

> The Iraqi government attacked too soon. Support was not made ready in advance. Germany and Italy were determined to make effective help available, [but] this failed on account of too rapid a collapse of the 'Iraqi will to resist and difficulties in transporting troops, weapons and supplies.[47]

This was a balanced assessment, correctly assigning a share of the blame to earlier Axis hesitation as well as to Iraqi incompetence. But it omitted what was possibly the decisive factor: the British government's firm resolve, despite the reluctance of its local military commander, not to give either Rashid 'Ali or the Axis time to remedy their mistakes. It was an occasion when Churchillian dash and determination paid handsome dividends.

One of General Wavell's principal objections to military action in Iraq, it will be recalled, was fear of the possible repercussions in the rest of the Arab world. In fact, events in Iraq appear to have had relatively little impact elsewhere in the Middle East, except for Syria, whence Engert reported on 4 May that they 'have had a deplorable effect . . . Even in circles which are not anti-British the belief is gaining ground that they may herald the decline and fall of British power and influence in the Middle East.'[48] In Egypt, Anwar as-Sadat's young officers appealed to the veteran nationalist, 'Aziz al-

[47] Unpublished record of the Keitel-Cavallero conversation deposited at the Ministry of Defence for the Navy, London.
[48] *F.R.U.S. 1941*, Vol. III, p. 701.

Misri, to help them 'make Egypt a second Iraq. Rashid 'Ali had given the signal for the war of liberation, it was our duty to rush to his aid.' But 'to our great surprise, 'Aziz al-Misri refused to share our enthusiasm. He received the news from Baghdad with scepticism. He said: "You don't know Iraqi politicians as well as I do!" '[49] If there was to be any salvation for Egypt, it lay not with Rashid 'Ali, but with Rommel and attempts were in fact made to smuggle 'Aziz al-Misri out of the country by air to German-controlled territory. But on the night of 15/16 May his plane crashed on take-off and he was later captured and interned by the Egyptian government. Another possible focus of sedition, former prime minister 'Ali Mahir, was exiled to his house in the country.

It was clearly Rommel's advance, too, which inspired King Farouk to approach the Germans on 14 April through his father-in-law, the Egyptian ambassador to Iran, with the message that 'he was [at] one with his people in the wish to see victorious German troops in Egypt as soon as possible as liberators from the unbearably brutal English yoke.'[50] But the king's isolation was amply illustrated by the fact that he was unable to send a representative to discuss cooperation with the Germans, as the latter had proposed, because, as his father-in-law explained:

1. The king was surrounded solely by politically unreliable elements in sympathy with England. 2. The Egyptian cabinet was a 'hostile' government for the king, and he had to be constantly on guard with its members. 3. The

---

[49] Anwar as-Sadat, *Revolt on the Nile*, New York, The John Day Company, 1957, p. 39.
[50] *D.G.F.P.*, Vol. XII, No. 350. The ambassador made it clear, however, that the welcome did not extend to the Italians. 'When the Italians . . . advanced successfully toward Egypt,' he said, 'the greatest worry of the Egyptian people was that the country would be occupied by the Italians. Therefore the Italian retreat had been welcomed. Now that the German troops stood victoriously at the Egyptian frontier the people were not only calm but longed for an occupation of the country, certain that the Germans were coming as liberators and not, like the Italians, as new oppressors.'

king had no one besides himself, his father-in-law, in whom
he had unlimited confidence. 4. The entirely safe channel
of communication through a special secret code between the
king and himself was the only one which the king had with
the outside world. 5. Even if there were another confi-
dential representative, his dispatches would not remain
secret from the English.[51]

One is forced to conclude that, despite Wavell's mis-
givings, the British had Egypt pretty well sewn up.

As the most independent country in the Arab world
and one whose ruler was a traditional rival of the pro-
British Hashimites, Saudi Arabia might have been expected to take advantage of the embarrassment caused
by the Rashid 'Ali revolt.[52] But this did not happen. The
Iraqi prime minister addressed two appeals for support
to King Ibn Sa'ud. The first was in April, to which the
king replied 'that Iraq should decisively reach agreement
with [Britain] . . . should avoid sedition and should
have no dealings with the government or individuals who
seek personal advantage to the detriment of Iraq interests.'[53] After fighting broke out in May, Rashid 'Ali sent
a personal envoy to the Saudi court, but King Ibn Sa'ud
'told him straight away that they had blundered and
made a big mistake in fighting Great Britain at such a
critical time, and that any difference of opinion between
themselves and Great Britain should have been solved
by peaceful means.' Indeed, he argued that Iraq was
'indebted to Great Britain' for her independence. He
added that he was 'a staunch friend of Great Britain' and
would have gone to her aid if he had had sufficient arms.
'With the exception of . . . Palestine, Great Britain did
nothing against the Arab interests and the present war
is one of life or death. So our duty is, if not able to help

[51] Ibid., No. 448.
[52] Ibn Sa'ud had driven Sharif Husayn out of his Hijaz homeland
in 1924 and annexed it to his own domain in the following year.
[53] CRS A1608, A41/1/1, Pt 20.

Great Britain, to be neutral.'[54] This account is probably somewhat overdrawn, but it remains true that Rashid 'Ali and his supporters received absolutely no encouragement from King Ibn Sa'ud.

Things might have been very different, however, if the British government had followed Wavell's advice and tried to negotiate with Rashid 'Ali. Apart from the possibilities of Axis intervention discussed in the conclusion, the feeling, which Engert had noted in Syria and which was undoubtedly present elsewhere, that British power and influence in the Middle East were on the decline would have been strengthened immeasurably by acceptance of the *fait accompli* of the Iraqi *coup*. Wavell was right to be concerned at the consequences of an unsuccessful attempt to overthrow Rashid 'Ali by force, but he did not seem to realize that inaction, which would inevitably have been interpreted as a sign of weakness, posed an equal threat. Even if there was only the slightest chance of success, therefore, the risk of armed intervention had to be run. Fortunately for Britain, the gamble paid off.

[54] K. S. Twitchell, *Saudi Arabia*, Princeton, Princeton University Press, 1947, pp 106-07. The quotations come from a letter to Mr Twitchell from the Saudi minister in London.

V

The Campaign in Syria

With the Axis onslaught in the Balkans and North Africa
and the Iraqi *coup*, Syria did not figure prominently in
the hierarchy of British preoccupations during the early
part of April 1941. But this was not the case with
the Free French. On 1 April General de Gaulle arrived
in Cairo for consultations with General Catroux and
Middle East Command and his memoirs make it clear
that Syria was uppermost in his mind. They also show
that in one crucial respect – suspicion of British designs
upon the mandate – his attitude was not so very different from that of the Vichy government which had condemned to him death as a traitor. 'Sooner or later we had
to go [to Syria]', he wrote. 'Once we are there, France
would have the opportunity of providing an important
contribution to the common effort. But if this opportunity
were lost, it would be the same with the position of
France. For if we supposed that the Axis would win,
they would be the masters there as elsewhere. If the
opposite happened, the English would take our place.
The authority of Free France had therefore to be extended to Damascus and Beirut as soon as events permitted.'[1] Such was the legacy of the bitter conflict over
spheres of influence in the Middle East which had
characterized Anglo-French relations in the aftermath
of the Skyes-Picot Agreement.[2]

De Gaulle did not intend merely to wait on events, but
to hurry them along. At an Anglo-Free French conference in Cairo on 15 April he said that he proposed to
capture Beirut, Damascus and the airfield at Rayaq with
Free French troops, believing that once this had been
accomplished, there would be little or no further resistance. However, he needed some British support in

[1] De Gaulle, *Mémoires*, p. 149.
[2] See above, p. 12

122

the form of lorries, tanks and aircraft. When the record of this conference was transmitted to London, Eden, the Foreign Secretary, commented that he was prepared to risk the unfavourable repercussions such an operation was bound to have upon British relations with Vichy, provided there was a guarantee of success. But the Chiefs of Staff objected that Wavell simply did not have the tanks or the aircraft to support de Gaulle's plan, and if he did, he would be using them elsewhere.

The Free French leader did not intend to be put off, however. From Brazzaville, where he had gone after leaving Cairo, he cabled his colleagues in London on 23 April expressing his intention to issue a declaration regarding the Levant states. This would say that the Free French were 'prepared to recognize the independence and sovereignty of Syria and the Lebanon and to unite with these states in 'a moral and military alliance which would assure their defence against any attack and, as a counterpart, would contribute to the preservation of France's general interests in the Orient.' Qualified representatives of the Syrian and Lebanese people would be invited to come to Brazzaville to negotiate on this basis.[3] The proposed declaration was evidently intended as a prelude to an invasion of the mandate, for two days later he drew up a detailed plan of military operations which he sent to Catroux. Once again, it required British support in the realm of transport, armour and air cover.

It was at about this time that British intelligence began to receive the first reports of a heavy concentration of German airborne forces in Greece and the islands. It seemed likely that Crete was the target, but no one could be 100 per cent sure that it was not Cyprus, Syria or Iraq, contingencies which were given added plausibility by the Rashid 'Ali *coup*. Even if Crete was the objective, moreover, there was the possibility that this was but the first step to other destinations. This refocused British attention upon Syria, and

---

[3] De Gaulle, *Mémoires*, pp 391-92.

on 27 April General Dill informed Wavell that the Foreign Office was instructing its Consul General in Beirut 'to warn General Dentz' of a possible airborne attack 'and ask what preparations he is taking to defend Syria.' Dill said that Dentz would 'probably reply that he will resist but will not ask us for aid. This will however give us the opportunity of offering to help him if Syria will fight . . . If Germans land in Syria and French can be induced to resist it would be greatly to our advantage to stiffen them to prevent advance on Palestine or Iraq.' Wavell was accordingly asked to specify what he could offer to assist Syria so that 'a firm offer ' could be made to Dentz.[4]

The final sentence of Dill's cable was a warning to the effect that it was 'inadvisable under these conditions to employ Free French forces unless asked for.' Although de Gaulle would undoubtedly have thought so, there was nothing more than military expediency in this observation. As we have already seen, the Chiefs-of-Staff did not consider that the British plus the Free French were strong enough to *take* Syria. But the British and the Vichy French might be strong enough to hold it. Given the bitter hostility between the Vichy and Free French, however, the latter were best left out of it. The British attitude could and did change in the face of Dentz's non-cooperation.

The War Cabinet in London decided to back up the approach to Dentz with a veiled threat to Vichy. This was to be conveyed through the United States government, which, unlike Britain, still maintained diplomatic representation in the temporary French capital. If the French accepted German demands which went beyond the armistice agreement, such as the landing of troops in Syria, ran the British note, they would in effect be participating in the war. 'Such participation would constitute a departure from the condition of passive capitulation in which France received from us our

[4] Connell, *Wavell*, p. 457.

guarantee to restore her independence and greatness.[5] It would [also] be impossible for us to maintain in any respect the distinction we have hitherto drawn between unoccupied and occupied France in the execution of our military plans.' But there was a piece of carrot as well as a stick. 'If, on the other hand, the French government would effectively resist these encroachments, we should give them the utmost assistance in our power. It should be possible to hold Syria against any forces which the Axis could bring against it in the near future.'[6] Churchill underlined the urgency of the situation in a personal message to President Roosevelt. 'If the German air force and troop carrier planes get installed in Syria,' he wrote, 'they will soon penetrate and poison both Iraq and Iran and threaten Palestine. . . . I feel Hitler may quite easily now gain vast advantages very cheaply and we are so fully engaged that we can do little or nothing to stop him spreading himself.'[7]

In the opinion of the American Under Secretary of State, Sumner Welles, however, the British warning ran the risk of provoking the very German demands upon Vichy which it was designed to thwart. After some discussion between London and Washington, therefore, it was finally decided to approach Vichy with a general expression of hope that it would not go beyond the armistice agreements and a general assurance of British support if it should choose to resist any requests to do so.

The American ambassador in Vichy, Admiral William D. Leahy, saw Marshal Pétain on 3 May. He reported that the latter 'stated that he does not intend to agree to any collaboration by France that is beyond the requirements of the armistice agreement', but that when he was

[5] See, for example, Churchill's statement of 23 June, 1940, Woodward, *British Foreign Policy*, Vol. I, p. 314.
[6] Ibid., Vol. II, pp 67-68.
[7] William L. Langer and S. Everett Gleason, *The Undeclared War 1940-1941*, New York, Harper and Brothers for the Council on Foreign Relations, 1953 (hereafter cited as Langer and Gleason, *Undeclared War*) p. 497.

told 'that the British government will give all the assistance in its power if German demands beyond the letter of the armistice agreement are effectively resisted, he said: "I am unable to make any comment on that." ' Leahy was convinced 'that there is no prospect whatever of getting any assistance for the British cause from the French military or naval forces at the present time or until a tangible British victory somewhere gives promise of the probable eventual defeat of Germany.'[8] He did not need to add that this possibility seemed a little remote at the moment.

In the meantime, the British commanders in the Middle East had replied to Dill's cable of 27 April, pointing out that they distrusted Dentz and could not agree to approaching him as this would reveal British weakness. Until the Australian troops who had returned from Greece could be re-equipped, the largest force which they could spare for Syria was a mechanized cavalry brigade, an artillery regiment and an infantry battalion. They could, moreover, only spare these if they did not have to send any forces to Iraq. The Chiefs-of-Staff duly replied 'that no definite offer of help should be made to General Dentz, but that if he resisted a German landing, by sea or air, all available British help would be given to him at once . . . Immediate air action should [also] be taken against any German descent.'[9]

Dentz had also been asked what he would do in the event of a German airborne landing. He replied that he would resist any incursions and that he had the capability to do so. But this did not prevent him from cabling Vichy on 30 April asking whether it was in fact government policy to resist the Germans. The Vichy war minister, General Huntziger, replied on 4 May:

> It is not impossible that you may shortly be faced with a German attempt to give assistance to Iraq. If formations of German aircraft should seek to land on your airfields or

[8] *F.R.U.S. 1941*, Vol. II, pp 161-62.
[9] Churchill, *Second World War*, Vol. III, p. 289.

should fly over your territory, it would be expedient to consider that France is not in the position of a neutral power with respect to Germany. It is not possible to treat the armed forces of Germany as hostile, but you would naturally oppose with force any intervention by the British forces . . .[10]

This was followed on the 6th by an order from Admiral Darlan to give German aircraft en route for Iraq 'every facility' to continue their journey. 'Have received and understood your messages', Dentz replied with unquestioning obedience. 'Am issuing orders as a result.'[11] So much for Marshal Pétain's assurances to Admiral Leahy.

We are in fact approaching the high-water mark of Vichy's collaboration with Germany during the Second World War. A few days after these exchanges with Dentz, Darlan went to Germany for discussions with Hitler and von Ribbentrop. At the conclusion of the final meeting with von Ribbentrop on 12 May, the German record stated categorically: 'The conversation ended with the position on both sides having been made completely clear, i.e., that Darlan was resolved to take the clear course of entering the war against England in the near future.' Darlan, of course, was acting in the conviction that a German victory was inevitable, and he wanted concessions in return for collaboration. As the record of his conversation with von Ribbentrop put it, 'he . . . asked for a manifestly accommodating attitude by Germany in one or two points, so that he could finally win over the French people for the new policy.'[12] Unfortunately, the 'one or two points' were to prove highly intractable.

The Free French were as aware as anyone else of the implications of a German airborne assault upon Syria. On 2 May Catroux told de Gaulle that if it occurred and Dentz resisted, he would 'get in touch with him in

[10] Kirk, *Middle East*, pp 92-93.
[11] Lipschits, *La Politique de la France*, p. 94.
[12] *D.G.F.P.*, Vol. XII, No. 499.

an attempt to get him to rally to Free France with an assurance that his position and powers would be confirmed. If he refused, I would try to obtain at least a cooperation agreement.' On the other hand, if the High Commissioner did not resist, but withdrew his forces into the Lebanon leaving Syria to the Germans, Catroux proposed 'to enter Syria, with the means at my disposal and, if possible, with British support, and rally as many [Vichy] troops as possible.'[13] This plan, which, like all the others put forward by the Free French, required British logistical and air support, was put to a meeting of senior British military and political representatives in Cairo on 5 May. According to Catroux, Sir Miles Lampson and Air Marshal Tedder, the RAF commander, were enthusiastic, but Wavell maintained that he could not spare enough troops. Indeed, he could spare none if he was required to send a force to Iraq. There was another reason for the commander-in-chief's caution, which he outlined in a message to London. Any attempt by the Free French to assume the leading role, he warned, would create great resentment among the French population of Syria.

Wavell's wariness on the subject of Syria was no more welcome to Churchill than his wariness about Iraq. 'A supreme effort must be made to prevent the Germans getting a footing in Syria with small forces and then using Syria as a jumping-off ground for the air domination of Iraq and Persia', he wrote in a minute for the Chiefs-of-Staff on 8 May. 'It is no use General Wavell being vexed at this disturbance on his eastern flanks . . . We ought to help in every way without minding what happens at Vichy.'[14] The question was discussed by the Defence Committee of the War Cabinet later the same day. In view of Wavell's shortage of troops and his reluctance to use the Free French, the deputy prime minister, Attlee, wondered whether Britain should not try and play the Arab card and come out in support of

[13] De Gaulle, *Mémoires*, pp 395-96.
[14] Churchill, *Second World War*, Vol. III, p. 289.

an Arab federation. Cold water was thrown on this suggestion from various quarters. The Secretary of State for the Colonies, Lord Moyne, said that inter-Arab rivalries made such an idea impossible and that if it was desired to conciliate Arab nationalism in the area, it would be far better for the Free French to implement the 1936 treaties with Syria and the Lebanon. Churchill, eager as ever for action, was of the opinion that 'the time has passed for trying to liquidate matters by promises to the Arabs' and that since military action was required and Britain had no troops herself, she would have to rely on the Free French.[15]

The prime minister's thesis carried the day and on 9 May he cabled Wavell:

> You will no doubt realize the grievous danger of Syria being captured by a few thousand Germans transported by air. Our information leads us to believe that Admiral Darlan has probably made some bargain to help the Germans to get in there.[16] In face of your evident feeling of lack of resources we can see no other course open than to furnish General Catroux with the necessary transport and let him and his Free French do their best at the moment they deem suitable, the RAF acting against German landings. Any improvement you can make on this would be welcome.[17]

Far from suggesting improvements, Wavell had already acted to kill Catroux's plan. On the same day as Churchill's cable, the British liaison officer with the Free French, Major-General Spears, was telling de Gaulle that 'in view of fresh commitments [i.e. Iraq] it will be impossible to provide transport for the Free French troops for a month at the very earliest . . . This means that no operations by them can be contemplated for the moment.' Spears added that Wavell saw no point in de

[15] Minutes of 26th Meeting of Defence Committee (Operations), 8 May, 1941, deposited at the Public Record Office, London.
[16] As we saw in the last chapter (above, pp 103-4), this information was correct in so far as stop-over facilities for German aircraft were concerned.
[17] Churchill, *Second World War*, Vol. III, p. 289.

Gaulle's returning to Cairo either now or in the near future, for 'in the absence of any obvious reasons for your return, a renewed visit might be in the nature of an anti-climax and detract from the success of your first visit.' De Gaulle angrily retorted that in view of the unilateral British decision regarding the use of his troops, he did not have the slightest intention of returning to Cairo, and on 12 May he ordered Catroux to leave the Middle East on account of 'the negative policy which our British allies have seen fit to adopt concerning us in the Orient.'[18]

This threat was never carried out as it was overtaken by events. Information began to reach London of the arrival of German planes in Syria on their way to Iraq and of preparations for the shipment of French war *matériel* from the mandate to the Iraqi rebels. On 12 May General Dentz made the devastating admission to the British Consul General in Damascus that while 'at present his instructions did not provide for German occupation of Syria . . . if those orders came he would obey them.'[19] On 14 May the Defence Committee authorized the bombing of German aircraft on Syrian airfields irrespective of the effect this would have upon relations with Vichy, and Eden announced this decision in the House of Commons on the following day.

From Cairo, General Spears informed de Gaulle on the 14th that Catroux and Wavell had agreed upon the following course of action:

(1) . . . General Catroux is to broadcast from Jerusalem informing the French in Syria of German penetration. His later propaganda will depend upon circumstances. (2) Catroux is to prepare leaflets which should be ready to be dropped over Syria on the nights of [15 and 16 May]. (3) The Free French now . . . in Palestine will remain there. They are on the railway and can be moved to the frontier rapidly. . . . (4) Should the response to the

[18] De Gaulle, *Documents*, pp 140-41; de Gaulle, *Mémoires*, p. 398.
[19] De Gaulle, *Documents*, p. 145.

propaganda be satisfactory, the Commander-in-Chief will
give the Free French all the support he can in view of the
circumstances at the time.

Point 4 was heavily qualified, but it was better than
nothing. Both Eden and Churchill appealed to de Gaulle
to allow Catroux to stay on in Palestine. On 15 May the
Free French leader replied exultantly to the prime
minister in English: '(1) Thank you. (2) Catroux remains in Palestine. (3) I shall go to Cairo soon. (4) You
will win the war.'[20]

It soon became clear, however, that Wavell had lost
none of his reluctance to assign a leading role to the
Free French. The issue came to a head on 18 May, when
Catroux came to him with a report that Dentz was planning to withdraw all his forces into the Lebanon and
hand over Syria to the Germans. Pending the latter's
arrival, Catroux argued, there would be a brief period
during which the road to Damascus would be open and
he asked Wavell to issue the order for an immediate
advance to take advantage of this unique opportunity.
Wavell, who did not believe the report in the first place,
refused, but did agree to discuss the matter further on
the following day. At this meeting he again declined to
order an immediate advance, whereupon Catroux asked
that the Free French forces at least be moved to the
Syrian frontier to test French and Arab reactions and to
take advantage of them if necessary.

Wavell disliked the proposal because of the political
effects he thought it would have upon the Arab population, and because of the administrative and tactical difficulties he felt would be involved. He would have preferred to implement a plan of his own, which he had
drawn up a few days earlier, and which called for a
daring attack on Beirut and Rayaq, rather upon Damascus, which he considered a military liability. He added
that while everyone was agreed on the dangers of a
German occupation of Syria, hasty action with weak

[20] Ibid., pp 147, 152.

forces would only create more problems. However, in view of the fact that de Gaulle was expected in Cairo on 24 May and a blank refusal to accede to Catroux's request would entail a break with the Free French, Wavell requested an immediate decision on whether he should agree to it in spite of his own reservations. If the answer was yes, he felt that a Free French declaration of independence for Syria, backed by the British government, should precede any military action.[21]

In spite of his assertion that 'all agreed . . . on the dangers of a German occupation of Syria', Catroux maintains that Wavell himself did not appreciate them, arguing that they were 'neither imminent nor mortal for Egypt.' This was in sharp contrast to Air Marshal Tedder, who 'declared that the possession of the Syrian platform would give the Axis powers aerial mastery of the Middle East.'[22] Tedder's account does not support Catroux's description of Wavell's attitude, although it does not contradict it either. It does, however, confirm Tedder's own position. After the meeting, he sent a private message to Air Chief Marshal Portal, the Chief of the Air Staff, saying that 'while it was not for me to say what could or could not be done from the army point of view, I felt it necessary to emphasize that the longer it was before action was taken the more dangerous did the situation become from the air point of view. If the enemy was allowed to establish his forces in Syria, the threat to Egypt, particularly the canal and Suez, to Iraq, and to our vital oil supplies from Abadan, became gravely increased. Our land communications from Palestine to Baghdad would become precarious since it would be impossible to provide effective air cover.' The bombing of the Syrian airfields had apparently had a favourable political effect, but 'air action alone . . . could clearly not maintain this political effect, and since land action was not possible we had to face the probability of a considerable enemy air force operating from Syria.'

[21] Connell, *Wavell*, pp 460-61.
[22] Catroux, *Dans la Bataille*, pp 125-26.

Tedder evidently shared Catroux's view that prompt
action was not only necessary, but had a good prospect
of success. 'Personally,' he noted in his journal, 'I believe
that two men and a boy could do *today* what it would
require a division to do in a couple of months' time.'[23]

There were also broader political considerations which
Eden set out in a long minute to the prime minister on
the same day, 19 May. Apart from the intrinsic importance of Iraq and Syria, he wrote, recent developments
in these two countries caused him 'most concern on
account of their influence on Turkey's policy. So far,
Turkey has held fast to the Anglo-Turkish alliance and,
for the present at least, appears to wish to continue to do
so. Our military attaché at Ankara reports that the Turks
are concentrating troops on the Iraqi and Syrian frontiers
and are asking us in return for our plans for dealing
with the situation in these recalcitrant countries.' The
foreign secretary thought it

> essential that we should make a plan of our own and that
> we should take the Turks to a large extent into our confi-
> dence . . . If once the Germans are able to establish them-
> selves in any strength in Syria and in Iraq, and succeed in
> organizing a part of the Arabs against us, Turkey will be
> effectively surrounded and it would indeed be difficult
> then to count upon her enduring loyalty . . . Taking a
> long view, there is this further consideration: if, as a result
> of her isolation, Turkey were to cave in and allow the
> passage of German troops into Syria, Germany would
> presumably be able to accumulate in due course important
> armoured forces in Syria and Iraq. These forces would
> not be limited by the difficulties of communication and
> supply which hamper any forces advancing on Egypt from
> the west, and a more formidable German army could
> then be maintained and employed from Syria than from
> Tripoli.[24] The only way to stop this is for Turkey to hold
> fast, and the only way to ensure that Turkey holds fast

[23] Marshal of the Royal Air Force Lord Tedder, *With Prejudice*,
London, Cassell, 1966, p. 93 (emphasis in original).
[24] This was very similar to the argument put by Mussolini to von
Ribbentrop only a few days before. See above, p. 105.

is to deal at the earliest possible moment with the situation in Syria and in Iraq.[25]

The situation in Iraq, of course, was being dealt with; but not that in Syria.

It was not surprising, therefore, that the Defence Committee agreed on 20 May to direct Wavell that:

> Catroux's request was to be granted; the Free French were to be given not only the transport they wanted but as much military and air support as possible; an immediate Free French declaration of independence for Syria and the Lebanon would be backed by Britain. The opportunity was too good to miss, and entering these two territories was to be regarded as a political *coup* rather than a military operation, and timing was all-important.

Apparently ignorant of Tedder's private message to Portal, Wavell was convinced that the Defence Committee's decision was the result of pressure from the Free French and their supporters, and was angry that they had been able to have his own views overruled. 'All reports from trustworthy sources including Arab and Syrian agree that effect of action by Free French alone likely to be failure', he protested. '. . . You must trust my judgment in this matter or relieve me of my command. I am not willing to accept that Catroux, de Gaulle or Spears should dictate action that is bound seriously to affect militarily situation in Middle East.'[26]

One can all the more readily sympathize with Wavell when one realizes the other heavy demands upon his resources. Iraq has already been discussed at length in the previous chapter, but this was a flea-bite compared with Crete, where the German assault had begun the previous day (20 May), and the Western Desert, where he was being urged to counter-attack as soon as possible with the help of tank reinforcements recently arrived

[25] The Rt. Hon. the Earl of Avon, *The Eden Memoirs: The Reckoning*, London, Cassell, 1965 (hereafter cited as Eden, *The Reckoning*), pp 246-247.
[26] Connell, *Wavell*, pp 461-62.

from England. Churchill underlined these other preoccupations by beginning his reply to Wavell's complaint with the words: 'Nothing in Syria must detract
at this moment from winning the battle of Crete, or
in Western Desert.' Nevertheless, he was to support
Catroux as ordered and was 'wrong in supposing that
policy arose out of any representations made by the
Free French leaders or General Spears. It arises entirely
from view taken here by those who have the supreme
direction of the war and policy in all theatres. Our view
is that if Germans can pick up Syria and Iraq with
petty forces, tourists and local revolts we must not
shrink from running equal small-scale military risks and
facing the possible aggravation of political dangers from
failure.' The prime minister was thoroughly exaspera-
ted with what he regarded as Wavell's undue caution
and he had already discussed his replacement. He was
therefore not in the least intimidated by Wavell's suggestion that he should be relieved if his judgement were
not accepted. 'For this decision', Churchill concluded,
'we are of course taking full responsibility, and should
you find yourself unwilling to give effect to it arrangements will be made to meet any wish you may express
to be relieved of your command.'[27]

Fresh information had meanwhile shown Catroux
what Wavell had suspected all along: namely, that his
'intelligence' concerning Dentz's withdrawal into the
Lebanon was false. Far from withdrawing, the Vichy
forces had occupied positions from which they clearly
intended to defend Syria against any British or Free
French incursion, and Catroux's plan for an advance
on Damascus with a small force was clearly no longer
practicable. In a telegram to the prime minister, Wavell
tactfully explained that it was the proven inaccuracy of
Free French information about Syria which had caused
him to fear a commitment at a time when multiple demands in Crete, Iraq and North Africa claimed all his

[27] Connell, *Wavell*, p. 462.

attention and resources. But he did not use these continuing emergencies as an excuse for opposing any action
in Syria. On the contrary, he appears to have been won
over by Tedder's air power considerations. 'This Syrian
business is disquieting,' he cabled on 22 May, 'since
German air force established in Syria are closer to the
Canal and Suez than they would be at Mersa Matruh.
. . . I am moving reinforcements to Palestine, after full
discussion with [my colleagues] . . . because we feel
we must be prepared for action against Syria, and weak
action is useless. The whole position in Middle East is
at present governed mainly by air-power and air bases.
Enemy air bases in Greece make our hold of Crete precarious, and enemy air bases in Cyrenaica, Crete, Cyprus,
and Syria would make our hold on Egypt difficult.'[28]
There was no more talk of resignation.

Three days later Wavell sent an outline of his plan
for the invasion of Syria, code-named EXPORTER, to
London. The invasion force, which would be commanded by General Wilson, would be ready to move in
the first week of June. Because of its small size, however, it could not hope to occupy the whole country. The
furthest it could reach was the line Beirut-Rayaq-Damas-
cus, with possible raids upon Tripoli and Homs. It
would not be able to take Aleppo, but Wavell wondered
whether the Turks could be induced to take that.

The Defence Committee examined Wavell's proposals
on 27 May. It met at a crucial stage of the war in the
Mediterranean, for the loss of Crete was imminent
and the Committee indeed confirmed Wavell's decision
to evacuate the island. Where would the Germans strike
next? General Dill was inclined to believe that they
would mount the famous pincer movement against
Egypt from the west and the north (through Turkey or
Syria), possibly taking in Cyprus on the way. In an
incisive minute on Dill's paper, Churchill commented:

. . . The defence of Egypt from the west and from the

28 Churchill, *Second World War*, Vol. III, p. 291.

north under the increased weight of the air attack from Crete presents the standard military problem of a central force resisting two attacks from opposite quarters. In this case the choice seems clearly dictated by the facts . . . The attack through Turkey and/or through Syria cannot develop in great strength for a good many weeks, during which events may make it impossible . . . In the Western Desert alone the opportunity for a decisive military success presents itself. Here the object must not be the pushing back of the enemy to any particular line or region, but the destruction of his armed force, or the bulk of it, in a decisive battle fought with our whole strength . . . There is no objection meanwhile to the advance he [Wavell] proposes . . . into Syria, and he may get the aerodromes there before the Germans have recovered from the immense drain upon their air-power which the unexpectedly vigorous resistance of Freyberg's army [in Crete] has produced . . . Forces should not be frittered away on Cyprus at this juncture. We cannot attempt to hold Cyprus unless we have the aerodromes in Syria. When we have these, and if we have gained a decisive victory in Cyrenaica, an advance under adequate air cover into Cyprus may become possible. We must not repeat in Cyprus the hard conditions of our fight in Crete.[29]

These views were approved by the Defence Committee and communicated to Wavell. It also accepted his suggestion to approach Turkey with a view to the occupation of northern Syria. Eden was aware that this would complicate Britain's relations with the Arabs, who would suspect that the Turks had come to stay, but he believed the risk worth taking, especially as he was by no means sure that the Turks would accept the invitation for fear of complicating their relations with the Germans. If this were so, Eden noted, 'our offer would have pleased them without doing any harm, though we should not get their active help.'[30] The foreign secretary's prediction proved accurate. The British ambassador in Ankara approached the Turkish foreign minister, Mr

[29] Churchill, *Second World War*, Vol. III, pp 684-85.
[30] Eden, *The Reckoning*, p. 247.

Saracoglu, on 2 June. On the following day 'Saracoglu brought up the question of Syria' in a conversation with von Papen. 'It was quite obvious', the latter reported, 'that they were afraid here of an English attack on Syria, which would perforce place Turkey under the necessity of taking over the Baghdad railroad and the area around Alep[po] for the strategic protection of her position. The minister intimated that he wished to speak with us about this question . . .' Von Ribbentrop promptly replied: '. . . We have no reason whatever to give any additional assurances beyond these advantages offered Turkey [in a draft treaty of friendship and non-aggression], such as, for example, with regard to Syria, which we cannot do in any case because of our relations with France. Turkish action against Syria would, moreover, naturally take place only in accord with England, and would thus be indirectly pointed against us . . .'[31] This information was conveyed to Saracoglu on 5 June and on the 6th he told the British ambassador that his government could not accept the British proposal to occupy northern Syria as this might involve it in war with France, and possibly Germany. The most it was prepared to do was to move troops to the Syrian frontier.

Despite the approval given to Operation EXPORTER, it very nearly did not take place as planned, owing to a combination of military and political factors. On the military side, there were some last-minute doubts as to the wisdom of proceeding. Alluding to Wavell's imminent counter-offensive in the Western Desert, Sir Alexander Cadogan, the permanent head of the Foreign Office, asked a meeting of top military and diplomatic advisers on 4 June: 'Why—a week before your effort in N[orth] Africa—do you blunder into a war with Vichy?' Of the same meeting, Eden records:

> We discussed Syria, pros and cons. There was much anxiety. Maybe we are too late for surprise and too early in the sense that our force is not large. Against this must

[31] *D.G.F.P.*, Vol. XII, Nos 586, 588.

be set the fact that it must be some time, a month at least, before our forces can be larger; meanwhile French will have time to consolidate, get their breath and German help. Vichy has sold out . . . A useful discussion, the general consensus being in the end in favour of going ahead with what must be a gamble.

The decision was endorsed by the Defence Committee on the following day. According to Cadogan, 'P.M. takes the cynical view that he has to face a debate on Crete on Tuesday. So we'd better begin the Syrian venture on Saturday and take the two together!'[32] If this was so, Churchill soon had cause to regret his flippancy. The counter-offensive in the Western Desert, by which he had set so much store, failed miserably, largely as a result of the dispersion of British forces caused by the simultaneous invasion of Syria. Wavell was the obvious scapegoat and on 21 June he was replaced as Commander-in-Chief, Middle East, by General Auchinleck, while he took up the latter's post in India.

On the political side, EXPORTER was almost prevented by a bitter wrangle between the British and Free French, which centred upon relations with the native population of Syria and the Lebanon. The British, who believed that Arab support was essential to the success of the campaign if the Vichy forces resisted, put considerable pressure upon the Free French to appease the nationalists. The Free French on the other hand regarded relations with the Arabs in the mandate as a matter for their exclusive concern, and regarded the British attempts to influence them as part of 'perfidious Albion's' sinister design to exclude France from the Middle East altogether.

The dispute was fought out over two issues: Catroux's designation and the proclamation of independence which it had long been agreed he would make to the Syrians and Lebanese at the outset of the campaign. On the

[32] Eden, *The Reckoning*, p. 249; David Dilks (Ed.), *The Diaries of Sir Alexander Cadogan, 1938-1945*, London, Cassell, 1971 (hereafter cited as *Cadogan Diaries*), p. 386.

first point, de Gaulle originally wanted to appoint Catroux as High Commissioner to succeed General Dentz, but the British government felt that this smacked too much of the discredited mandatory regime and eventually persuaded him to use the term Delegate-General and Plenipotentiary instead.

On the second point, Catroux's first draft, according to General Wilson, only offered 'independence with reservations', whereas the British wanted 'freedom for Syria without reservations and . . . a constitution [for the Lebanon] subject to French interests and the guarding of minorities . . .' It was also felt that the Jebel Druze should be given the opportunity to be autonomous and that any statement must be 'clear and unambiguous.'[33] This disagreement seems to have been resolved, but the British then demanded the right to associate themselves with the proclamation. The rationale of this proposal, which, it will be recalled, had been suggested by Wavell, is not at all clear, but it implied considerable doubt as to the good faith of the Free French. De Gaulle believed it was deliberately designed 'to create the impression that, if the Syrians and Lebanese obtained independence, they owed it to England, and [the British] . . . wanted to put themselves in the position afterwards of arbiters between us and the Levant states.'[34] He succeeded in avoiding anything in the nature of a joint document, but he could not prevent the British from issuing a parallel declaration of their own supporting Catroux's proclamation. The incident boded ill for the future.

In his proclamation, which was broadcast on 8 June, 1941, the day allied forces (Australian, British and Free French) crossed into Syria, Catroux assumed 'the powers, responsibilities and duties of France's representative in the Levant.' 'In this capacity,' he said, 'I come to put an end to the mandatory régime and to proclaim you free and independent. You will henceforth be sovereign

[33] Wilson, *Eight Years*, p. 110.
[34] De Gaulle, *Mémoires*, p. 160.

and independent peoples and you can either form your-
selves into separate states or join together in one single
state. In either case, your independent and sovereign
status will be guaranteed by a treaty in which our re-
ciprocal rights will be defined.' As a result of this proclamation, he continued, the Syrian and Lebanese people
would know that the allied forces had not come to suppress their freedom, but to assure it. Their purpose 'is
to chase Hitler's forces from Syria. It is to prevent the
Levant from becoming a base of enemy offensive operations against the British or against ourselves'.[35]

It is ironic that these justifications of the allied invasion had lost most of their validity by 8 June. After
the collapse of the revolt in Iraq, the Vichy government
quite understandably began to worry that its help to
the Axis powers would bring down British wrath upon
Syria. In a letter to Otto Abetz, the German ambassador
in France, on 1 June, Admiral Darlan wrote:

> The reports which I have received from Syria since Iraq
> has sued for an armistice cause me to fear the possibility
> of an English attack against the Levant countries and in
> any case an intensification of de Gaullist activity and of
> English propaganda. . . . In order to deprive such an attack
> in advance of any pretext, it is of the greatest importance
> that German aircraft and German personnel returning
> from Iraq not stay in Syria . . . I would therefore urgently
> request you to intervene with the German high command
> with a view to ordering the evacuation of personnel and
> of German and Italian air force material sent to the
> Levant since 9 May.[36]

Hitler took the point, and far from ordering a build-
up of German forces in Syria to prepare for an attack
upon Egypt, as the British feared, he gave instructions
for all units to leave the country with the exception of
a small liaison mission attached to the Italian armistice
commission. When the invasion began, the French asked
for the withdrawal of this mission as well on the grounds

[35] Woodward, *British Foreign Policy*, Vol. I, pp 584-85.
[36] *D.G.F.P.*, Vol. XII, No. 581.

that it might lead public opinion to believe that the Germans had not given up the idea of turning Syria into a military base, and once again Hitler obliged, fearing 'that the French will probably not be able to hold Syria in any case, and that therefore the right thing to do is to withdraw the German personnel there in time.'[37]

The German action in withdrawing their forces from Syria enabled the Vichy government to adopt a holier-than-thou posture in the face of the Anglo-Free French invasion. 'If the British think that they are going to stop a German drive on Suez by conquering Syria they are gravely mistaken,' Admiral Darlan told Admiral Leahy on 12 June, 'for the Germans have never planned to use Syria in their major operation.' On the other hand, Darlan went on, there were documents in French possession dating back six months which proved conclusively that the British were planning to invade Syria even then. 'In fact', he said, echoing General de Gaulle's own deepest suspicions, 'they always wanted Syria.'[38]

Neither the British nor the Free French seem to have realized the extent of the German withdrawal. But, in any event, they could always argue that the Germans might return. This was indeed the firm belief of Rudolf Rahn, the German foreign ministry representative in Syria, who stayed on during the fighting. '. . . I secretly persisted in the conviction that a German intervention in Syria would come sooner or later,' he wrote in a retrospective report on his activities at the end of July, 'since, in the circumstances, relief for Rommel's army seemed feasible only from Syria.' Even after the invasion of the Soviet Union, which tied up the bulk of Germany's resources and about which he had evidently not been informed in advance, Rahn clung to his belief. '. . . I was convinced,' he wrote, '. . . that the English would attempt a thrust through Iran to the oil fields of Baku and that this could be prevented or, at any rate, seriously im-

[37] Ibid., No. 606.
[38] *F.R.U.S. 1941*, Vol. III, p. 737.

peded, from Syria, if we wanted to avoid a break with Turkey.'[39]

Rahn's masters, however, never even contemplated the kind of large-scale commitment he envisaged, at least not before the successful completion of Operation BARBAROSSA.[40] Indeed, Russia loomed so large upon their horizons that it was hard to obtain a hearing for the claims of an actual theatre of operations like North Africa, let alone for those of a potential one like Syria. Besides, French resistance was not expected to last for very long. Hitler's opinion to this effect has already been quoted, and von Ribbentrop expressed the same view to Ciano on 15 June, although one week's fierce fighting had shown that Dentz's army was no walk-over.

The only kind of direct assistance the Axis powers were prepared to consider was air support. The idea seems to have originated with General de Giorgis, the chairman of the Italian armistice commission in Syria. On the second day of the fighting he told Dentz that he had suggested to Rome that the Italian air force should attack Palestine and that Rome had asked for the High Commissioner's views. Dentz replied that, as far as he was concerned, the Italian air force could attack the British wherever it liked, so long as it did not use Syrian airfields. Somehow, the Germans got hold of the idea that it was Dentz who had requested air support and informed the French delegaton to the armistice commission on 10 June that they were prepared to act, not only in Palestine and Syrian coastal waters, but also, according to circumstances, in the combat zone itself.

In a telegram to Dentz and the French delegation on the following day, General Huntziger set out the Vichy government's position quite clearly.

> For reasons of morale [he wrote] the intervention of the German air force will have to take place without over-flight of the Levant territories . . . The British fleet supporting the land attack off the Lebanese coast is the most

[39] *D.G.F.P.*, Vol. XIII, No. 165.
[40] For post-BARBAROSSA planning, see below, pp 161-62.

interesting target for us at the moment . . . Other targets which are equally important for current operations are the airfields at Amman, Haifa and Lydda, as well as the Haifa port installations . . . A possible target is British convoys from Haifa to Cyprus . . . In so far as intervention in the immediate combat zone is concerned, this cannot take place except upon representations by General Dentz.[41]

On the same day, however, Admiral Goutton, the Vichy naval commander in the Levant, urged Dentz to drop his opposition to German aircraft using Syrian airfields. The High Commissioner agreed and cabled Vichy on 12 June:

The constant bombardment by the British fleet, on the one hand, and on the other, the rather rapid wastage of my troops, which I cannot replace from my meagre strength, have changed my views concerning the intervention of German aircraft. Request permission for a squadron of German aircraft, intended to intervene against British fleet or for land operations, to use Aleppo airfield. Have informed R[ahn].[42]

The latter enthusiastically seconded Dentz's proposal. As he explained in his July report, '. . . It seemed to me to be the beginning of a logical chain: First the French would ask for German help against the fleet, then against the motorized English troops; finally they would gladly reconcile themselves to a commitment of German ground forces.'[43]

But Vichy replied that it was sending a squadron of French aircraft to attack the British fleet and that the use of German planes could only be contemplated if it was 'not merely speedy and sustained, but also massive.' Could Dentz fulfil the necessary technical conditions for such intervention? The High Commissioner had to

[41] *La Délégation Française auprès de la Commission Allemande d'Armistice: Receuil de Documents publié par le Gouvernement Français*, Volume IV, Paris, Alfred Costes/Imprimerie Nationale, 1957 (hereafter cited as *La Délégation Française*), p. 542.
[42] Kirk, *Middle East*, p. 99.
[43] *D.G.F.P.*, Vol. XIII, No. 165.

admit that he could not. 'Massive and sustained support would involve placing at disposal of German air force defensive material or airfield services which I cannot supply', he replied. 'The Germans would thus be led to occupy the whole of north Syria.'[44] Later the same day, 13 June, the *Luftwaffe* notified the armistice commission that it could not provide effective support without using Syrian airfields.

The reasons for Vichy's reluctance to re-admit the *Luftwaffe* to Syria were frankly put to the Germans. On 10 June Baron Jacques Benoist-Méchin, Admiral Darlan's State Secretary, told the head of the German delegation to the armistice commission that while German air attacks upon Palestine, and particularly Haifa, could be of considerable help in the defence of Syria: 'the French command cannot take the initiative because of the serious political consequences which possible English reprisals against any part of our territory could have. This would mean the extension of the conflict, which, on the contrary, must be localized in view of the present state of our forces.'[45] Darlan himself made much the same point to Abetz six days later when he said that 'an open employment of German [air force] units in Syria could automatically unleash English attacks against Morocco and West Africa and the reinforcements necessary for the defence of these colonies were not yet all in position. He would therefore like to request the *Reich* government for the direct help of German aircraft only when Syria could not be held by any other means.'[46]

For Dentz, however, local military considerations continued to make the use of German aircraft desirable. After a visit to Damascus on 15 June, he telegraphed Vichy that the use of *Stukas* (Junkers Ju 87s) based in Syria against land as well as naval targets would be decisive. In response, Vichy sent out its air minister,

[44] Kirk, *Middle East*, p. 99.
[45] *La Délégation Française*, p. 570.
[46] G.F.M., 658, 256776-77.

General Bergeret, on a mission of examination and explanation. He and the local air force commander drafted a joint telegram, signed by the latter, which was sent to Vichy to coincide with his return. It opposed the commitment of German aircraft from Syrian bases for three reasons:

> 1. Stocks of war materials, petrol, and bombs, would not allow us to give German formations the help and defence which they would be compelled to request if they were called in. 2. I consider that the general moral situation of France imposes on French forces in Syria the duty to fight alone without the help of foreign forces admitted into Syria. 3. The support requested would perhaps be effective against the enemy fleet, but would not decisively shape the outcome of the land battle. It would therefore compromise us seriously without compensating advantage. Better to go down alone than with another.[47]

After the war it was alleged by those involved that the Vichy air crews had made it quite plain that they did not want to fight alongside the Germans, but there is no contemporary documentary evidence of this.

Pétain and Darlan freely admitted that their forces could not hold Syria on their own. Why, then, did they go on fighting? Abetz provided the answer in a report to Berlin on 11 June. 'The French government considers that Syria's moral will to resist has been proved', he wrote. 'Today [the Syrian army] . . . is ready to sacrifice itself in a struggle against English attacks, hopeless though it may be, because it believes that by this demonstration of loyalty to Germany it can improve the position of metropolitan France and the rest of the colonial empire for the duration of the armistice treaty and in the peace treaty.'[48] The battle for Syria took place, in fact, at the very same time as the comprehensive negotiations between Germany and Vichy France foreshadowed at the time of the Darlan-Hitler-von Ribbentrop meeting

[47] Kirk, *Middle East*, p. 100.
[48] *D.G.F.P.*, Vol. XII, No. 616.

in mid-May, and the relationship between the two events was understood by everyone, in Syria as well as at Vichy. When Dentz indignantly told Rahn on the day of the allied invasion: 'Now the Near East is aflame, and it is you who have set it ablaze', the German replied: 'Are not the French northern provinces worth more than ten Syrias?'[49] Dentz could only agree. 'You know, indeed, that I shall fight', he said, '– and to the last man.' Similarly, when he was told by General Bergeret on 18 June that the Franco-German negotiations were deadlocked, he exclaimed bitterly to Rahn: 'Tell me, what are we fighting for here anyway?' The German was able to calm him and even thought he had succeeded in convincing him 'that the principal blame for the impasse . . . lay with the French.' However, he went on, 'the fighting spirit of the general staff was temporarily paralysed. On June 21 Damascus fell without any apparent necessity, and the political director of the High Commissioner told me . . . "The fall of Damascus bears the name of Bergeret." '[50]

Bergeret's gloomy tidings were probably also the cause of the first feelers for an armistice. On 18 June M. Conty, the same political director mentioned above, had asked Engert to enquire of the British, 'as it were on [Engert's] own initiative', about possible terms for a cease-fire. He referred to reports that the Free French had sentenced Dentz and other senior officers to death and said that such 'jests' were not conducive to an atmosphere of negotiation. He was therefore particularly anxious to know what the British and the Free French really intended to do about the French army in the Levant, the French civil administration, and all other Frenchmen and their families. Although he did not say

[49] The French *départements* of the Nord and the Pas-de-Calais were attached to the German military administration in Belgium and it was one of the Vichy government's objectives in the negotiations with Germany to have them restored to France.
[50] *D.G.F.P.*, Vol. XIII, No. 165.

so, Engert commented, Conty was clearly speaking on Dentz's behalf.[51]

The British government replied on 19 June that it 'would be very ready to consider satisfactory arrangements whereby our strategical requirements in Syria are fully safeguarded. Far from desiring to impose any dishonourable terms on General Dentz His Majesty's Government are fully prepared to accord full honours of war to him and other civilian and military officers who have only done what they conceived to be their duty by their government . . . There is therefore no question of General Dentz or any other civilian or military official being condemned to death or to any other penalty.'[52] The British reply also included a detailed outline of the military clauses of an armistice, but Engert suggested that since Conty had not specifically requested these and had confined himself to the political aspects of a cease-fire, the communication of this outline could await a firm French decision to negotiate. The British government agreed to this procedure on 21 June, but hinted that the armistice terms might get tougher as time went on.

Engert saw Conty again on 25 June. Whether as a result of Rahn's pep-talks or other factors, Conty told the American that 'the French authorities did not feel the time had come to negotiate. And when I said the terms might not be quite the same later he replied peevishly he could not help that. He said the British military effort had been so feeble that at this rate it would take them two months to occupy Syria and by that time "the Germans will wipe up the floor with them and occupy Jerusalem within forty-eight hours." '[53]

[51] *F.R.U.S., 1941*, Vol. III, pp 743-44. Engert was the obvious choice as an intermediary after the expulsion of the British consuls in Beirut and Damascus in mid-May.
[52] *F.R.U.S., 1941*, Vol. III, pp 745-46.
[53] Ibid., p. 750. Thanks to the tenacity of the Vichy resistance, the allied advance had indeed been slower than anticipated. The original plan expressed the hope that Damascus and Beirut would be reached on the first day of the fighting, but as we have seen, Damascus was not taken until 21 June and Beirut was not taken at all, although the Australians were only five miles from it at

De Gaulle's reaction to the British terms was no less explosive than Conty's. He had been consulted at the time of the latter's original approach and, together with Lampson and Wavell, had worked out a set of terms which did not differ greatly from those transmitted to Engert except in so far as they included several explicit references to the role and rights of the Free French. But there was no mention at all of the Free French in the terms handed over to Conty and de Gaulle angrily cabled Eden on 20 June that he was astonished at Britain's unilateral action 'in a matter in which Free France and the lives of Free French soldiers are involved as well as England and the lives of British soldiers, and in respect of questions which essentially concern the future of French military and civilian personnel and the fate of territories over which the authority of France is exercised.' Britain's behaviour was all the more unpardonable as Conty had specifically asked for Free French as well as British views. In the circumstances, de Gaulle declared, he did not feel bound in any way by the terms as delivered.[54]

Eden's reply was unconvincing. 'In drafting these terms,' he cabled Lampson on 22 June, 'we took fully into account the views expressed to us by General de Gaulle and the Commander-in-Chief, Middle East . . . We had also in mind great accession of strength to Free French which would result if Syria could be promptly secured as a result of American offer [to mediate]. It therefore seemed unnecessary to refer text of our telegram to Washington to the Commander-in-Chief and

---

the time of the cease-fire. In the second half of June General Wilson summoned up a two-pronged supporting attack from the east: HABFORCE, which was to take Palmyra and then advance on Homs and Tripoli; and the 10th Indian Division (also from Iraq), which was to advance up the Euphrates and take Aleppo. HABFORCE reached Palmyra on 23 June, but did not succeed in taking it until 3 July, while the 10th Indian Division took Raqqa on the 5th. But Homs, Tripoli and Aleppo were still in Vichy hands at the time of the armistice.

[54] De Gaulle, *Mémoires*, pp 428-29.

General de Gaulle, as terms were virtually identical and
the matter brooked of no delay.'[55] But this completely
missed the point of de Gaulle's complaint, which was
concerned precisely with the *difference* between the two
sets of terms: namely, the omission of any reference to
the Free French. One cannot help suspecting, in fact,
that this omission was quite deliberate and reflected a
British assessment that any mention of the Free French
would only make a settlement harder to obtain, given
Vichy's bitter hostility to de Gaulle.

For the latter, this incident was just one more example of the British tendency to ride roughshod over
French rights. Another was their attitude towards relations with the Arabs in Syria and the Lebanon. In a
telegram to his colleagues in London on 1 July, he
warned of possible opposition to Free French rule in
the mandate from 'a team of Arab sympathizers' attached
to Middle East Command, the British embassy in Cairo
and the Palestine High Commission. These people had
'always intrigued against France in Arab countries and
are apparently disposed to continue.' He had sent
Churchill 'a very clear telegram' on this subject and
urged his colleagues to show, in their relations with the
British and particularly with the Foreign Office, that all
were equally concerned.[56]

In the telegram to Churchill, which was sent on 28
June, de Gaulle emphasized that 'the manner in which
British policy proceeds in respect of Syria will be a very
important criterion . . . If, to the satisfaction of Vichy,
Berlin and Rome, our joint action in Syria and the
Lebanon appeared to result in a diminution of the position of France and the introduction of purely British
tendencies and activity, I am convinced that the effect
upon opinion in my country would be disastrous. I must
add that my own efforts, which consist in maintaining,
both morally and materially, French resistance against
our enemies at England's side, would be seriously com-

[55] De Gaulle, *Documents*, p. 174.
[56] De Gaulle, *Mémoires*, p. 433.

promised as a result.' He was sure that Churchill shared this view, but expressed the hope that all the local British authorities would also act in accordance with the same principle. He did not want the impression to be created 'that the occupation of Syria by troops who were in part British and under a British commander involved either a shift in authority to the detriment of France or some sort of supervision of France's authority.'[57]

On this point, Vichy's view was much the same. It seems that the Pétain-Darlan government was not informed of Conty's approach to Engert and the British reply until 26 June, when Dentz sent two officers back to France to explain the situation and to point out that a continuation of the struggle was impossible. The response was a communication to Admiral Leahy on 30 June which stated that 'the French government is disposed to authorize General Dentz to enter into contact with General . . . Wilson to examine conditions for the cessation of military operations' provided that 'the proposed negotiations imply the recognition by the British government of the maintenance of all the rights and prerogatives that the mandate guarantees to France over the whole of the territory of Syria and the Lebanon' and that 'the principle of the agreement should be the fixing of a line of demarcation . . . to the south of which the British command would have the powers which are recognized by international law to an occupying force.' To the north of the proposed demarcation line, it was implied, the Vichy authorities would continue to rule.[58]

Commenting on this proposal in a telegram to Dentz, General Huntziger said that the French negotiating

---

[57] De Gaulle, *Mémoires*, p. 432.
[58] *F.R.U.S., 1941*, Vol. III, pp 755-56. This approach had been cleared with the Germans who, while stating their conviction that British intentions were insincere and that France would therefore be well advised not to make an agreement with them, nevertheless 'added . . . that if the French considered themselves incapable of offering further resistance, we naturally would have to leave to them the final decision as to how they should proceed.' (*D.G.F.P.*, Vol. XIII, No. 101.)

position would be 'all the better to the extent that our resistance continues to make itself felt; a few days gained can have a capital importance.'[59] But Huntziger's promise of accelerated reinforcements to enable Dentz to fulfil this task could not be kept. Benoist-Méchin, who had arrived in Ankara on 24 June on a special mission to persuade the Turkish government to allow the passage of war matériel through its territory left virtually empty-handed on 2 July. At one point, in fact, it looked as though the Turks would ask Vichy to grant them a 'trusteeship' over Syria until the end of the war, but Benoist-Méchin and Papen 'agreed that discussion of such an idea was unacceptable as long as the possibility to defend Syria existed and that furthermore a Syria under Turkish trusteeship would be far more inconvenient to Germany's conduct of the war later on' – presumably after the successful conclusion of Operation BARBAROSSA – 'than a Syria in British hands.'[60] Another possibility of prolonging resistance remained the use of the *Luftwaffe*. Indeed, Dentz made a final appeal for this on 1 July, pointing to the recent large-scale reinforcement of the RAF in his theatre. But Vichy continued to oppose any suggestion that German planes should operate from Syrian bases and it was only on this condition that the *Luftwaffe* was prepared to consider intervening.

When the British rejected the proposed partition of Syria on 7 July, therefore, the Vichy government authorized Dentz to begin negotiations with the British for a ceasefire whenever he deemed it necessary. The High Commissioner approached Engert the following day and the American handed him the British terms on the 11th. This time they were those which de Gaulle had approved and Engert reported that Dentz 'seemed anything but pleased. He snorted audibly every time he came across a reference to Free French interests and said it was "disgraceful and outrageous of Great Britain to

[59] *La Délégation Française*, p. 538.
[60] *D.G.F.P.*, Vol. XIII, No. 71.

encourage Frenchmen to engage in civil war." He
added that he would have no dealings with the Free
French but would deal exclusively with the British
and all French officials . . . had been instructed to do
likewise.'[61]

Vichy rejected the terms on the grounds that recognition of Syrian and Lebanese independence according
to the Catroux declaration was 'incompatible with [its]
rights and prerogatives as mandatory power' and that it
could not 'lend itself under any pretext whatsoever to
negotiations with Frenchmen who are traitors to their
country like De Gaulle and Catroux.'[62] But Dentz was
nonetheless authorized to conclude a purely military
agreement and hostilities ceased on the night of 11/12
July as a prelude to it. Dentz had been urged, by Rahn
as well as by his own government, to agree to nothing
which would enhance the position and prestige of the
Free French and his representatives certainly succeeded
in carrying out this instruction during the three days
of negotiations at Saint Jean d'Acre from 12 to 14 July.
The armistice, which was signed on the 14th, contained
no reference to the Free French. It was not even signed
by them, although Catroux was present throughout the
negotiations. Any Vichy war *matériel* which was not
destroyed was to be handed over to the British and not
the Free French, although the latter had a desperate need
of equipment. The locally recruited *troupes spéciales,*
who were not permitted to serve outside the mandate,
were to be placed under British and not Free French
command. Finally, and this was a most important point
as far as the Free French were concerned, the provisions
enabling the Vichy troops and administrators to opt
whether to join de Gaulle or be repatriated to France
were feeble in the extreme. The Free French had wanted
to separate the Pétainist officer corps from the other
ranks and to be able to proselytize freely, but there
was no mention of this. Indeed, no contract between

[61] *F.R.U.S., 1941*, Vol. III, p. 770.
[62] Ibid., pp 771-72.

the Free French and their fellow-countrymen was
permitted.

General de Gaulle was understandably furious at the
outcome, which he described in his memoirs as 'equiva-
lent to a pure and simple handing over of Syria and the
Lebanon to the British.'[63] He upbraided Catroux, who
subsequently and unconvincingly claimed that he was
unaware of de Gaulle's views, for agreeing to the armistice and on 21 July bluntly informed the newly appointed
British Minister of State in the Middle East, Oliver
Lyttleton, that 'Free France, that is to say, France' was
not bound in any way by the armistice agreement and
that he intended to withdraw all Free French forces from
British command in three days' time.[64] This threat, like
that of Catroux's withdrawal from the Middle East two
months earlier, was not carried out because Lyttleton and
de Gaulle managed to work out an agreement which
'interpreted' the armistice to the satisfaction of both
parties. The Vichy war *matériel* was to be handed over
to the Free French and the *troupes spéciales* were to
be incorporated into their forces. The right to proselytize
the Vichy troops was a little more difficult to arrange,
for, unlike the other concessions, it required the consent
of the other party to the armistice. However, it was
decided to impose it as a 'sanction' for breaches of the
agreement by the Vichy side and the Free French were
eventually able to rally almost 6,000 out of a total of
37,750 troops and about one-third of the 1,200 civilian
officials.

A more long-term problem was Arab nationalism.
Despite appeals from both sides, the urban nationalists
had remained quiescent during the fighting. Rahn's attitude towards them was nothing short of contemptuous.
'. . . I found nothing in Syria that would have been
capable of militant action', he wrote. 'At the moment of
danger, they all failed, the swaggering leaders of the
Arab freedom movement. In undisguised anxiety, they

[63] De Gaulle, *Mémoires*, p. 164.
[64] Ibid., p. 446.

asked for our assistance in fleeing abroad, if they had not already preferred "as a precaution" to make contact with the English . . . After long and laborious efforts, I had to give up working with the old, national groups.'[65]

It was de Gaulle's original intention to revert to the position in July 1939, when Puaux had suspended the Syrian constitution, and to take the 1936 treaty as the point of departure for fresh negotiations with the Syrian leaders. He therefore called upon Hashim al-Atasi, Jamil Mardam and Faris al-Khuri (respectively president, prime minister and president of the Chamber of Deputies in July 1939) to begin discussions with him and General Catroux. But, as he records in his memoirs, he found these gentlemen 'too concerned to my mind with legal formalities and too susceptible to the suggestions of a contrary nationalism.'[66] As a result, the Free French were compelled to set up an interim government under Sheikh Taj ad-Din al-Hasani, a Francophile who did not enjoy anything like the support that Atasi would have had. In the Lebanon, the rivalry of the leading politicians gave them an excuse to retain Dentz's appointee, Alfred Naqqash, in power.

British policy towards the political future of Syria was set out by Churchill in the House of Commons on 9 September, 1941:

We have no ambitions in Syria. We do not seek to replace or supplant France, or substitute British for French interests in any part of Syria. We are only in Syria in order to win the war. However, I must make it quite clear that our policy, to which our Free French allies have subscribed, is that Syria shall be handed back to the Syrians, who will assume at the earliest possible moment their independent sovereign rights. We do not propose that this process of creating an independent Syrian government, or governments—because it may be that they will not be one government—shall wait until the end of the war. We con-

[65] *D.G.F.P.*, Vol. XIII, No. 165. One of the nationalists who left Syria before the Anglo-Free French takeover was Shukri al-Quwwatli.
[66] De Gaulle, *Mémoires*, p. 177.

template constantly increasing the Syrian share in the administration. There is no question of France maintaining the same position which she exercised in Syria before the war, but which the French government had realized must come to an end. On the other hand, we recognize that among all the nations of Europe the position of France in Syria is one of special privilege, and that in so far as any European countries have influence in Syria, that of France will be pre-eminent.[67]

But de Gaulle was not so sure. 'There is at work in this country,' he had telegraphed his colleagues in London on 12 August, 'a tenacious group of British Arab sympathizers supported by the prime minister and the Colonial Office. These Arab sympathizers have seen in the Syrian affair an opportunity to chase France out.[68] One of the 'Arab sympathizers' most criticized by the Free French was Major Glubb. He has admitted that he carried out anti-French propaganda in Syria, but claims that this was because he was not properly informed of British government policy. 'In the preparatory work undertaken before the invasion of Syria,' he writes,

it had been assumed by one and all that French control of Syria was at an end . . . Both British and Arabs assumed that Syria would be controlled by Great Britain until the end of the war, and would then become independent in the same manner as Iraq. It was, therefore, with no little surprise and consternation that we heard that the French were to continue to govern Syria . . . Presumably in London the Free French had been promised the control of Syria before the invasion commenced. Apparently the commanders in the Middle East were not aware of the promise. Certain it is that no mention of it was made to us. Before the invasion, we were told to place ourselves in touch with the Syrians to ensure that they would not support the Vichy French against the British forces . . . Such propaganda inevitably took the form of the liberation of Syria from French control.[69]

[67] House of Commons Debates, 5th series, Vol. 374, col. 76.
[68] De Gaulle, *Mémoires*, p. 468.
[69] Glubb, *Arab Legion*, pp 344-45. Glubb's activities probably

Lack of coordination undoubtedly accounted for some of the tension between Britain and Free France in 1941, but there was a more fundamental reason. The Rashid 'Ali revolt seems to have convinced the British government that it must display more sympathy towards Arab nationalism if it was to maintain its own position in the Middle East. One symptom of this was Eden's cautious public endorsement of pan-Arabism in his speech at the Mansion House in London on 29 May, 1941:

> The Arab world has made great strides since the settlement reached at the end of the last war, and many Arab thinkers desire for the Arab peoples a greater degree of unity than they now enjoy. In reaching out towards this unity they hope for our support. No such appeal from our friends should go unanswered. It seems to me both natural and right that the cultural and economic ties between the Arab countries, yes, and the political ties, too, should be strengthened. His Majesty's Government, for their part, will give their full support to any scheme that commands general approval.[70]

This was later translated into backing for the Arab League, which took shape under Egyptian leadership between 1943 and 1945.

As far as Syria and the Lebanon were concerned, the British policy took the form of unrelenting pressure upon the Free French to implement, in deed as well as in word, their pledge of independence for the two countries. This naturally encouraged the nationalists and led to periodic confrontations between them and the French authorities, culminating in a serious outbreak of violence in Damascus in May 1945 which was only brought to

---

also reflected the ambitions of his immediate employer, the Amir 'Abdullah, who had never made any secret of his desire to avenge the eviction of his brother Faysal from Damascus by the French 21 years earlier by ascending the throne of Syria himself. Mr Lyttleton had to make a special visit to Amman to make it clear to the Amir that it was not British policy that he should become king of Syria.

[70] Anthony Eden, *Freedom and Order*, London, Faber & Faber, 1947, p. 105.

an end by the intervention of British forces, who confined French troops to their barracks under threat of military action. In the light of these events, Churchill's repeated denials that Britain wished to usurp France's position in the area sounded more unconvincing than ever. But they were probably true. It was not French predominance as such which was being attacked, but what were felt to be the inflexible methods by which it was being perpetuated and which threatened to turn Syria and the Lebanon into a festering sore which, like Iraq in 1941, might infect the rest of the (British-controlled) Middle East.

In retrospect it is easy to see that the policy was a mistake. Apart from embittering Anglo-French relations, it did little to appease the Arab nationalists, who could only contrast British solicitude for their rights in Syria and the Lebanon with their disregard for them in Egypt and Iraq. Arab resentment was compounded when Britain, largely as a result of American pressure, failed to prevent the creation of the Jewish state of Israel in 1948. The twin pillars of the British position in the Middle East – Egypt and Iraq – crumbled in the 1950s just as surely as those of France in Syria and the Lebanon in the 1940s. In 1952 the 'free officers' seized power in Egypt. They comprised the same men who, eleven and twelve years earlier, had supported 'Ali Mahir and tried to smuggle 'Aziz al-Misri out of the country. The withdrawal of British troops was negotiated in 1954 and the ill-fated Suez expedition of 1956 showed that they could never successfully return. Iraq, where the faithful Nuri as-Sa'id continued to dominate the political scene, remained in the British orbit until 1958. But on 14 July of that year the young King Faysal, 'Abd al-Ilah and Nuri himself were brutally murdered in the aftermath of a military *coup*. One of the first acts of the new régime was to permit the return of the exiled Rashid 'Ali to Baghdad.

The Strategic Implications

In terms of men and resources involved, the 1941 campaigns in Iraq and Syria were on a very small scale. Moreover, they were and have remained ever since, largely overshadowed by contemporary events in North Africa, Greece, Crete and the Soviet Union. It is even possible, in the light of what we now know about Hitler's intentions, to argue that, from an overall strategic point of view, the campaigns were unnecessary. German eyes were fixed upon Russia, such an argument runs, and British fears of a gigantic pincer movement against Egypt from the north and west, making use of Iraq and/ or Syria, were a figment of their imagination. Both countries could therefore have been left to stew in their own juice until Rommel's army in North Africa had been destroyed, rather as Wavell had appeared to favour.

But this, of course, is an argument from hindsight. It is not generally realized just how late it was before the British were *certain* – and not merely aware of the possibility – that Germany would attack the Soviet Union. Admittedly, Churchill has maintained that he foresaw what was in the offing as early as the end of March 1941. Referring to intelligence information at this time concerning 'the movement and counter-movement of German armour on the railway from Bucharest to Cracow', he has written: 'To me it illuminated the whole Eastern scene like a lightning-flash. The sudden movement to Cracow of so much armour needed in the Balkan sphere could only mean Hitler's intention to invade Russia in May. This seemed to me henceforward certainly his major purpose. The fact that the Belgrade revolution had required their return to Romania involved perhaps a delay from May to June.'[1]

---

[1] Churchill, *Second World War*, Vol. III, p. 319.

Such was not the view of everyone, however, as
Churchill himself admitted. As late as 31 May, Sir
Alexander Cadogan recorded in his diary: 'Chiefs-of-
Staff have come to conclusion that Germany is *prepared*
to attack Russia. I agree, but *I* believe that Russia will
give way and sign on the dotted line. I wish she wouldn't,
as I should love to see Germany expending her strength
there. But they're not such fools (as *our* General Staff).
But we must consider how we can use threat or fact of
bombing to Baku.'[2] This was the origin of the telegram
sent to Wavell later the same day which read

> We have had firm indication that Germans are now con-
> centrating large army and air forces against Russia. Under
> this threat they will probably demand concessions most
> injurious to us. If the Russians refuse the Germans will
> march. Russian resistance may be strongly influenced if
> they think that should they submit to Germans we shall
> attack Baku oil. If we are to use this threat . . . we must
> control Mosul before Russians and/or Germans can fore-
> stall us. Most energetic action should therefore be taken
> to get control in Mosul.[3]

In other words, even after the campaign in Iraq was
as good as over, the permanent head of the Foreign
Office, the Chiefs-of-Staff, and presumably the War
Cabinet too, believed that the concentration of German
forces on Russia's borders could simply be designed to
pressure her into making concessions and might well
succeed in that objective. Indeed, it was only on 12
June, ten days before the invasion began and four days
after the beginning of the Syrian campaign, that the
inter-departmental Joint Intelligence Committee emphatically concluded that 'fresh evidence is now at hand
that Hitler has made up his mind to have done with
Soviet obstruction and to attack.'[4] In the circumstances,
it would obviously have been foolish for the British to
have disregarded the possibility of a German invasion of

[2] *Cadogan Diaries*, p. 382 (emphasis in original).
[3] Connell, *Wavell*, p. 446.
[4] Churchill, *Second World War*, Vol. III, p. 318.

the Middle East through Turkey, Syria and/or Iraq, even though it did not in fact take place.

Even if the British had been certain that Hitler was about to attack the Soviet Union, they would still have been most unwise to have ignored the dangers in Iraq and Syria, even momentarily. In the first place, they felt that, given the dispersal of British forces, it would not have required a tremendous diversion of Axis resources to have snapped up both countries. Secondly, while the endurance and heroism of the Soviet resistance to the German invasion is now a matter of record, not many predicted such a long and bitter struggle at the time. 'Our advisers were pessimistic about what the Russians could do', Eden has recorded. 'Cripps [the British ambassador in Moscow] excused the Soviet appeasement of the Nazis on the grounds of their extreme weakness. Every day must count for them. He had told the War Cabinet on June 16th that the prevailing view in diplomatic circles in Moscow was that Russia could not hold out against Germany for more than three or four weeks. Dill, in conversation with me, hoped for a few weeks longer, but thought we should be unwise to count on more than six or seven.'[5] Once the Germans had smashed the Soviet Union, it was only to be expected that they would re-direct their attention to the Middle East, and if Iraq and Syria were in pro-Axis hands, they would have had a good base upon which to build.

Germany certainly entertained plans along these lines. Draft military directive No. 32 of 30 June, 1941, entitled 'Preparations for the time after BARBAROSSA', spoke of the 'continuation of the *struggle against the British position in the Mediterranean and the Near East* by means of a concentric attack which is to be launched from Libya through Egypt, from Bulgaria through Turkey, and possibly from Transcaucasia through Iran' as one of the 'strategic tasks for the *Wehrmacht* [which] can arise for the late autumn of 1941 and winter 1941-

[5] Eden, *The Reckoning*, p. 269.

1942.' The draft went on to say that 'in the case of [these] . . . operations, the situation of the English in the Middle East will be all the more difficult the more forces are tied down *at the proper time*[6] by centres of unrest or insurrectionary movements.' As 'all military, political, and propaganda measures serving this purpose must be harmonized very closely with one another in the preparatory period', the directive designated General Felmy's Special Staff F, which had been set up under military directive No. 30 in the form of a military mission to Iraq, 'as the central office in the field to participate in all planning and measures in the Arab area. It is to be given the best experts and agents.'[7]

On 24 July, 1941 Field-Marshal von Brauchitsch, the commander-in-chief of the German army, sent the OKW a detailed plan for these operations. In the case of the advance through Turkey, Brauchitsch said that the army had no evidence to support the assumption that the Turks would not resist. It would therefore require a large force (five armoured divisions, three motorized divisions and twelve infantry divisions) and could not be mounted until 1942. If Turkey was prepared to cooperate, on the other hand, this force could be reduced by half and the operation carried out at the turn of 1941/42. Spring of 1942 was the deadline for the operation from Transcaucasia through Iran to the Persian Gulf. It would require one reinforced armoured corps and some mountain troops. It will be noted that these plans were drawn up after the collapse of all resistance in Iraq and Syria. If these two countries had been subject to Axis influence, the deadlines and force levels would presumably have been correspondingly modified.

Russian resistance and the entry of the United States into the war had completely transformed the situation by the time even the first of the existing deadlines was reached and the plans were shelved. Things would have been very different, however, had Hitler chosen to

[6] This is presumably a reference to the premature Iraqi revolt.
[7] *D.G.F.P.*, Vol. XII, No. 617 (emphasis in original).

concentrate his forces against the Middle East in 1941. In a note written at about the time of the German invasion of the Soviet Union, a British military planner declared:

> Whether we can now hold on to the Middle East depends on one thing and one thing alone – whether the Germans concentrate seriously against us there. If they do, they will be able to develop their attacks in considerable strength from the west through Libya, from the north through Turkey, and possibly from the north-east through the Caucasus and Persia. We cannot produce sufficient strength in the Middle East in the near future to secure our position in face of serious attack from even one of these fronts. Even if we had the forces available for dispatch to the Middle East, which we have not, we have not the shipping to transport them or maintain them. The fact of the matter is that the maintenance of the forces already in the Middle East constitutes a drain on our resources which we can ill afford in face of the threat to the British Isles and to ill-defended key points, in particular, West Africa and Malaya. If we hold on in the Middle East over an appreciable period it will therefore be only because the Germans are fully occupied elsewhere.[8]

This quotation underlines the fact that it is not British, but German strategy which is usually criticized in respect of events in Iraq and Syria in 1941. If Britain did in fact have no need to fear an Axis pincer movement against Egypt in that year, was this not a cardinal error of German policy?

In what it subsequently described as 'one of the most important documents of the war records',[9] the German naval staff did outline an alternative strategy to that of concentration upon Operation BARBAROSSA. This was in a memorandum by Admiral Kurt Assmann of the naval war staff which dealt with the strategic situation and future operations in the eastern Mediterranean

[8] Major-General Sir John Kennedy, *The Business of War*, London, Hutchinson, 1957 (hereafter cited as Kennedy, *Business of War*), p. 137.
[9] Nuremberg Document 170-C, Item 168.

after the conclusion of the Balkan campaign and the occupation of Crete. Assmann wrote that:

> The British power position in the eastern Mediterranean is under the severest pressure as a result of the Balkan campaign and the occupation of Crete, but it is . . . not yet broken. All the signs indicate, moreover, that the British are in no way inclined to give up their position in the eastern Mediterranean. On the contrary, England appears determined to maintain her position in this area by every means. This is based, as in all other areas of decisive importance for the British Empire, upon the exercise of control of the sea by the British battle fleet . . . It alone is in the position to protect the maritime lines of communication which are essential for the control of the eastern Mediterranean position and to secure the power political influence in Egypt, Palestine, Iraq and to a considerable extent in Turkey, with its ramifications in the African, Indian and even the Far Eastern regions. Upon its shoulders, too, rests the prestige of the British Empire in the eastern Mediterranean. As always, therefore, it remains the aim of German-Italian strategy to destroy the British fleet as the controlling factor, to drive it out of the eastern Mediterranean and to eliminate its bases and operational possibilities in the Mediterranean.

In order to do this, Assmann argued, the naval war staff believed that it was not sufficient merely to hold the important strategic positions that had been gained 'but to make use of them energetically, methodically and with the greatest urgency for positive *offensive action* against the British position in the eastern Mediterranean.' While recognizing the importance of Operation BARBAR-OSSA, Assmann believed that it 'should . . . on no account lead to an abandonment, a diminution or a postponement of operations in the eastern Mediterranean. On the contrary, in the opinion of the naval war staff, *everything* must be attempted in order firmly to grasp the initiative in the eastern Mediterranean and to continue and intensify the struggle with powerful, energetic blows.'

Assmann then listed the various forms of pressure
which could and should be applied to the British in the
area. In respect of Syria – and it must be remembered
that his memorandum was written before the British
invasion – he urged that France be both permitted and
encouraged to strengthen the mandate's defences to
such an extent that a British attack would be ruled out.
In addition, there should be an 'examination of the
possibilities for the German *Luftwaffe* to operate from
Syrian territory against the Suez Canal and maritime
communications in the Red Sea (including aerial mine-
laying) as well as against supplying traffic to and from
Cyprus . . . [and] preparation of the military potential
for a possible subsequent support of a German offensive
against the British power position in the Middle East.'

> As always [he concluded] the naval war staff is convinced
> that control of the eastern Mediterranean and the com-
> plete elimination of any English political and military
> mark of strength in this area, with its important ramifica-
> tions in the entire Near East, is of such decisive importance
> for the overall conduct of the war that, in spite of other
> considerable demands upon the German armed forces
> (BARBAROSSA), all current problems in the area must be
> energetically tackled and all operational possibilities at
> present available unconditionally utilized in order to be
> able to exploit to the full the considerable successes recently
> obtained in the Mediterranean at a time when the help of
> the United States to England has yet to reach decisive
> proportions.[10]

One of the troubles with Assmann's memorandum
was that it was written rather late in the day. Thus it
was used as one of the briefing papers for Grand
Admiral Raeder's conference with Hitler on 6 June,
1941, when it was far too late to effect a major change
in Germany's strategy. Indeed, the memorandum strikes
one more as a 'statement for the record' than a positive
call for action. Raeder seems to have thought as much,

[10] Unpublished memorandum deposited at the Foreign and Commonwealth Office Library, London (emphasis in original).

for he only gave an abbreviated summary of the document to the Fuehrer, concentrating upon its recommendations for increased Italian activity in the Mediterranean.

Even as a statement for the record, however, the memorandum has its faults. Two years after it was written, Assmann remarked that it did not go the whole hog and propose that BARBAROSSA be abandoned in favour of operations in the eastern Mediterranean. One suspects that he thought this was a mistake and it is certainly hard to see how Germany could have carried out both the invasion of the Soviet Union and the offensive action in the eastern Mediterranean advocated by the navy with the resources at her disposal, particularly in the form of air power. The only alternative was to rely upon the Italians, but as Assmann was the first to admit, they were incapable 'of bringing the necessary operations in the Mediterranean to a successful conclusion with the necessary toughness, speed and penetration'. His solution was to employ 'German planning, German organization and stricter German leadership' with a good leavening of German forces, but it is doubtful whether this would have been enough.

It is possible, for example, as Churchill claims, that a different employment of their airborne forces in May 1941 'would have given [the Germans] . . . Syria, Iraq, and Persia . . .'[11] But would they have been able to hold them? Supply difficulties were an important factor in the defeat of both Rashid 'Ali and the Vichy French and they would have been exacerbated by the presence of even small German fighting units. Although Turkey would in all probability have succumbed to German pressure and permitted overland transit, control of the area ultimately rested, as Assmann pointed out, upon maritime communications in the eastern Mediterranean and these would not be secure until the British fleet was destroyed. It would have required more than a few airborne troops to accomplish this task.

[11] Churchill, *Second World War*, Vol. III, p. 236.

Let us assume, therefore, that the Germans had decided to take advantage of the situation in Iraq and Syria in the spring of 1941 to commit their strength massively in the eastern Mediterranean instead of against the Soviet Union. It is likely that they would have swept the British out of the Middle East, from Egypt to Iran, within a matter of months. This would have brought them considerable strategic advantages. They would have been threatening the British position in eastern and southern Africa and in India. They would have outflanked Russia to the south and been dangerously close to her Caucasian oil fields. Not least, they would have acquired oil fields of their own in Iraq and Iran, which, as stated earlier,[12] produced sufficient oil in 1941 to cover Germany's actual consumption during that year, including six months' *Blitzkrieg* in the Soviet Union. Shortage of oil was one of the limiting factors upon Germany's, and still more Italy's,[13] capacity to wage war. Control of the major oil fields of the Middle East would have eliminated that problem.

But this does not necessarily mean that Germany would thereby have won the war. As it happened, the implications of the loss of Egypt and the Middle East were discussed in some detail by the British at the end of April and the beginning of May 1941 and the conclusions were not so categorical. The discussion arose out of Churchill's quite sudden discovery that General Wavell had drafted a contingency plan covering a withdrawal from Egypt. The prime minister regarded this as rank defeatism and on 28 April wrote a directive to the Chiefs-of-Staff in which he stated that 'the loss of Egypt and the Middle East would be a disaster of the first magnitude to Great Britain, second only to successful invasion and final conquest . . . It is to be impressed upon all ranks, especially the highest, that the life and honour of Great Britain depends upon the successful

[12] See above, p. 23.
[13] The Italian navy's fuel stocks ran out in June 1941, which meant that thenceforth it could only conduct operations as and when fresh supplies of oil arrived.

defence of Egypt . . . All plans for evacuation of Egypt or for closing or destroying the Suez Canal are to be called in and kept under the strict personal control of Headquarters. No whisper of such plans is to be allowed . . . The Army of the Nile is to fight with no thought of retreat or withdrawal.'[14]

In their reply of 7 May, the Chiefs-of-Staff 'entirely agree[d] that "the loss of Egypt . . . would be a disaster of the first magnitude", and . . . would welcome an exhortation to the Army of the Nile that they are "to fight with no thought of retreat or withdrawal" ', but they felt that it was 'an overstatement to say that "the life . . . of Great Britain depends upon the successful defence of Egypt." Surely our life continues so long as we are not successfully invaded, and do not lose the Battle of the Atlantic.' They agreed that contingency plans such as Wavell's should be known to only a few, and this was in fact the case. At the same time, they thought 'it necessary that these plans should be continually revised and kept up to date. However confident we may be of victory, it would be tempting providence to disregard the possibility of a reverse.'[15]

General Dill had already written some personal comments on the previous day:

The loss of Egypt would be a calamity which I do not regard as likely, and one which we would not accept without a most desperate fight; but it would not end the war. A successful invasion alone spells our final defeat. It is the United Kingdom therefore and not Egypt that is vital, and the defence of the United Kingdom must take first place. Egypt is not even second in order of priority, for it has been an accepted principle in our strategy that in the last resort the security of Singapore comes before that of Egypt. Yet the defences of Singapore are still considerably below standard . . . Risks must of course be taken in war, . . . they must be calculated risks. We must not fall into the error of whittling away the security of vital points. If

---

[14] Butler, *Grand Strategy*, pp 577-78.
[15] Ibid., pp 578-79.

need be, we must cut our losses in places that are not vital before it is too late.[16]

Churchill was not convinced. Replying to Dill's paper on 13 May, he wrote: 'I gather you would be prepared to face the loss of Egypt and the Nile Valley, together with the surrender or ruin of the Army of half a million we have concentrated there, rather than lose Singapore. I do not take that view, nor do I think the alternative is likely to present itself.' The Chief of the Imperial General Staff's 'truisms' about calculated risks depended 'entirely upon their application to circumstances' and he hoped that the reference to cutting losses in places that were not vital was 'not intended to have any relevance to the present situation in Egypt.'[17]

But Dill, too, was unrepentant. On 15 May he told the prime minister that he agreed that 'the alternative of losing Egypt or losing Singapore is not likely to present itself.' He believed that the German advance in the Middle East had been stemmed. 'But it is possible that it may not prove to be so. In this unlikely event of our having to withdraw from Egypt, I do not think we should be faced with the surrender or ruin of an army of half a million. A great proportion of the half million in the Middle East are not in the Nile Valley. I hope that we should be able to withdraw in good order a large proportion of the fighting personnel and equipment to hold the Germans on the next line of resistance, and to advance again when the enemy in his turn was forced to fall back, as he certainly would be in the end.' As for the relevance of his remarks about cutting losses in Egypt, he 'certainly intended to imply that if we reach a point when the maintenance of our position in Egypt would endanger either the United Kingdom or Singapore, we should hold fast to the two latter, even if this meant the loss of Egypt. That is my considered opinion, and it is, I think, in line with your own ideas as expressed

[16] Churchill, *Second World War*, Vol. III, p. 375.
[17] Churchill, *Second World War*, Vol. III, pp 376-77.

in your memorandum of 17 November, 1939.'[18]

It was not only Churchill's military advisers who were questioning the priority accorded to the Middle East, but his friends across the Atlantic. In a cable to the British prime minister on 1 May 1941, President Roosevelt argued that the British had 'fought a wholly justified delaying action' in Greece and would 'continue to do so in other parts of the Eastern Mediterranean, including North Africa and the Near East.' But 'if additional withdrawals become necessary they will all be a part of the plan which at this stage of the war shortens British lines, greatly extends the Axis lines, and compels the enemy to expend great quantities of men and equipment. I am satisfied that both here and in Britain public opinion is growing to realize that even if you have to withdraw farther in the Eastern Mediterranean you will not allow any great *débâcle* or surrender, and that in the last analysis the naval control of the Indian Ocean and the Atlantic Ocean will in time win the war.'[19]

Churchill replied three days later:

We must not be too sure that the consequences of the loss of Egypt and the Middle East would not be grave. It would seriously increase the hazards of the Atlantic and the Pacific, and could hardly fail to prolong the war, with all the suffering and military dangers that this would entail. We shall fight on whatever happens, but please remember that the attitude of Spain, Vichy, Turkey, and Japan may be finally determined by the outcome of the struggle in this theatre of war. I cannot take the view that the loss of Egypt and the Middle East would be a mere preliminary to the successful maintenance of a prolonged oceanic war. If all Europe, the greater part of Asia and Africa, became, either by conquest or agreement under duress, a part of the Axis system, a war maintained by the British Isles, United States, Canada, and Australasia against this mighty agglomeration would be a hard, long, and bleak proposition.[20]

[18] Butler, *Grand Strategy*, p. 581.
[19] Churchill, *Second World War*, Vol. III, p. 208.
[20] Churchill, *Second World War*, Vol. III, p. 208.

Roosevelt replied on 10 May that his previous remarks 'merely meant to indicate that should the Mediterranean prove in the last analysis to be an impossible battleground, I do not feel that such a fact alone would mean the defeat of our mutual interests. I say this because I believe the outcome of this struggle is going to be decided in the Atlantic and unless Hitler can win there, he cannot win anywhere in the world in the end.'[21]

All these exchanges took place before the German invasion of the Soviet Union. But, presumably because of their equally low estimate of Russian chances of survival, this event did nothing to alter the American view. In July Roosevelt's personal adviser, Harry Hopkins, came to London. He told the British 'that the chief military advisers in the USA hold the opinion that our Middle East policy is a mistaken one. They think our position there is quite hopeless, and that to send further reinforcements there is like " throwing snowballs into hell". As a result of this, he feels that the USA will not be willing to provide large numbers of tanks, etc, if we mean to allot them to the Middle East . . . He says that they would prefer to keep the equipment for themselves rather than let it go to the Middle East.'[22] American military representatives in London, in fact, rated the defence of the Middle East fourth, below (in descending order) the defence of the United Kingdom and the Atlantic sea lanes, the defence of Singapore and the sea lanes to Australia and New Zealand, and the defence of the ocean trade routes in general. Despite their own views cited earlier, the Chiefs of Staff apparently managed to convince them that the Middle East was more important than that.

In the event, the British retained Egypt and the Middle East, lost Singapore, and still won the war. The resistance of the Soviet Union and the assistance of the United States were of course the decisive factors in the ultimate victory rather than the loss or retention of any

[21] Langer and Gleason, *Undeclared War*, p. 418.
[22] Kennedy, *Business of War*, p. 153.

area outside the United Kingdom itself, and if one assumes, as it seems one must, that a German concentration upon the Middle East in 1941 would have delayed rather than averted a Nazi-Soviet confrontation, then the final outcome would probably have been the same. But the shape of the war would have been very different and its duration considerably prolonged.

BIBLIOGRAPHY

Books and published works

As-Sadat, Anwar: *Revolt on the Nile*, New York, The John Day Co., 1957.

Avon, the Earl of: *The Eden Memoirs: The Reckoning*, London, Cassell, 1965 (see also under Eden).

Be'eri, Eliezer: *Army Officers in Arab Politics and Society*, London, Pall Mall, 1969.

Butler, J. R. M.: *Grand Strategy*, Volume II, London, HMSO, 1957.

Catroux, Georges: *Dans la bataille de Méditerranée: Egypte-Levant-Afrique Du Nord 1940-1944*, Paris, Julliard, 1949.

Churchill, Winston S.: *The Second World War* (6 volumes), London, Cassell, 1948-54.

Connell, John: *Auchinleck*, London, Cassell, 1959. *Wavell: Scholar and Soldier*, London, Collins, 1964.

De Chair, Somerset: *The Golden Carpet*, London, Faber and Faber, 1944.

DeGaulle, Charles: *Mémoires de Guerre*, Volume I, *L'Appel 1940-1942*, Paris, Plon, 1954.
War Memoirs, Volume I, *The Call to Honour 1940-1942: Documents*, London, Collins, 1955.

Dilks, David (Ed.): *The Diaries of Sir Alexander Cadogan 1938-1945*, London, Cassell, 1966.

Evans, Trefor, E. (Ed.): *The Killearn Diaries, 1934-1946*, London, Sidgwick and Jackson, 1972.*

Eden, Anthony: *Freedom and Order*, London, Faber and Faber, 1947.

Glubb, John Bagot: *The Story of the Arab Legion*, London, Hodder and Stoughton, 1948.

Halder, Generaloberst Franz: *Kriegstagebuch*, Volume II, Stuttgart, W. Kohlhammer Verlag, 1963.

Hirszcowicz, Lukasz: *The Third Reich and the Arab East*, London, Routledge and Kegan Paul, 1966.

Hourani, Albert H.: *Syria and Lebanon: A Political Essay*, London, Oxford University Press for the Royal Institute of International Affairs, 1946.

Hytier, Adrienne D.: *Two Years of French Foreign Policy: Vichy 1940-42*, Paris/Geneva, Librairie E. Droz, 1958.

KEDOURIE, Elie: *The Chatham House Version and other Middle Eastern studies*, London, Weidenfeld and Nicolson, 1970.

KENNEDY, Sir John: *The Business of War*, London, Hutchinson, 1957.

KHADDURI, Majid: *Independent Iraq 1932-1958*, London, Oxford University Press for the Royal Institute of International Affairs, 1960.

KIRK, George: *The Middle East in the War*, London, Oxford University Press for the Royal Institute of International Affairs, 1952.

LANGER, William L., and Gleason, S. Everett: *The Undeclared War 1940-1941*, New York, Harper Brothers for the Council on Foreign Relations, 1953.

LIPSCHITS, Isaac: *La Politique de la France au Levant 1939-1941*, Paris, Editions A. Pedone, 1963.

LONG, Gavin: *Greece, Crete and Syria*, Canberra, Australian War Memorial, 1953.

MONROE, Elizabeth: *Britain's Moment in the Middle East 1914-1956*, London, Chatto and Windus, 1963.

MUGGERIDGE, Malcolm (Ed.): *Ciano's Diplomatic Papers*, London, Odhams, 1948.

PAL, Dharm: *Campaign in Western Asia*, New Delhi, Orient Longmans, 1957.

PLAYFAIR, I. S. O.: The Mediterranean and the Middle *East*, Volumes I and II, London, HMSO, 1954, 1956.

SACHAR, Howard M.: *Europe Leaves the Middle East, 1936-1954*, New York, Alfred A. Knopf, 1972.*

TEDDER, Marshal of the RAF the Lord: *With Prejudice*, London, Cassell, 1966.

TWITCHELL, K. S.: *Saudi Arabia*, Princeton, Princeton University Press, 1947.

WEIZMANN, Chaim: *Trial and Error*, London, Hamish Hamilton, 1949.

WILSON OF LIBYA, Field-Marshal the Lord: *Eight Years Overseas, 1939-1947*, London, Hutchinson, 1949.

WOODWARD, Sir Llewellyn: *British Foreign Policy in the Second World War* (5 volumes), London, HMSO, 1970-in progress.

* These books were only seen by the author after the completion of this study.

Bibliography

Documents and official sources

Archives of the Commonwealth of Australia, Series A1608.
Brassey's Naval Annual 1948, London, William Clowes, 1948.
Documents on German Foreign Policy, Series D (1937-45), 13 volumes, London, HMSO, 1949-64. Relevant volumes X, XI, XII, XIII.
Foreign Relations of the United States, Diplomatic Papers, Washington, U.S. Government Printing Office, 1870-in progress. Relevant volumes, 1940, III; 1941, II, III.
German Foreign Ministry Records (unpublished) deposited at the Foreign and Commonwealth Office, London.
House of Commons Debates, 5th series. Relevant volumes 358, 374.
I Documenti Diplomatici Italiani, 9th series, Rome, La Libreria dello Stato, 1952-in progress. Relevant volumes IV, V.
La Délégation Française auprès de la Commission Allemande d'Armistice: Recueil de Documents publié par le Gouvernement Français, Volume IV, Paris, Alfred Costes/Imprimerie Nationale, 1957.
Minutes of 26th Meeting of Defence Committee (Operations), 8 May, 1941, in the Public Record Office, London.
Nuremberg Documents 170-C, 1776-PS.
OKW directive (unpublished) deposited at the Ministry of Defence for the Navy, London.
Record (unpublished) of the Keitel-Cavallero conversation deposited at the Ministry of Defence for the Navy, London.
Report (unpublished) of the German military attaché in Rome deposited at the Imperial War Museum, London.

INDEX

Abadan, 23, 110-11, 132
'Abd al-Ilah, Amir, 35, 91, 117, 158
'Abdullah, Amir of Transjordan, 12-13, 34, 86, 112
Abetz, Otto, 141, 145-6
Abwehr, 41, 82, 84, 95
Aden, 24, 52, 111
Afghanistan, 83
Africa, 81, 167
Afrika Corps, 67
Al Qantara, 56
Alawi minorities, 13, 14
Aleppo, 13, 106, 116, 136, 138, 144, 149n.
Alexandria, 115
'Ali Mahir Pasha, 24-7, 36, 119, 158
Amman, 86, 144
Anatolia, 61
Anfuso, Filippo, 54
Anglo-Egyptian Treaty, 1936, 16, 25, 27, 39, 70
Anglo-Iraqi Treaty, 1930, 14, 16, 23, 36, 91-2
Ankara, 34, 37, 52, 85, 100, 108, 137, 152
Anwar as-Sadat, 27, 118
Arab Federation, 44, 82
Arab Higher Committee, 17-18, 43
Arab League, 157
Arab Legion, 72, 112-13
Arab nationalism(ts), 11, 13, 15, 16, 19-20, 29, 34-5, 38-9, 41, 43, 54, 78, 80, 154, 157, 158
Arab Revolt, 12
Arabia, 92
Arabs, 11-12, 17, 19, 39-40, 43-7, 52-5, 60, 70, 74, 80, 82, 85, 105, 110, 120, 131, 139
Assmann, Admiral Kurt, 164-7
Assyrians, 13
Attlee, Clement, 1st Earl, 128
Auchinleck, Sir Claude John Eyre, 86, 91-2, 110, 139
Australasia, 171
Axis powers, 19-20, 22-3, 31, 38, 45, 83, 92, 94, 98, 118, 122, 125, 132, 141; policy of, 39-42, 49-50, 57
'Aziz al-Misri, 25, 118-19, 158

Baghdad, 14, 19, 24, 31, 36, 43, 45, 48, 54, 55, 56, 64, 65, 66, 78, 86, 101, 105, 110, 111-12, 116-17, 119, 132, 138, 158; riots in Jewish quarter of, 117
Bahrein, 92
Bakr Sidqi *coup*, 35
Baku, 142, 160
'Balfour Declaration', 16
Balkans, *see* individual countries
Bardia, 67
Basra, 14, 23, 65, 83, 86, 90-2, 98, 99, 100, 102, 107, 109, 111-12
Battle of the Atlantic, 168
Battle of France, 30
Beirut, 18, 56, 122, 131, 136, 148n.
Belgrade, 89
Benghazi, 67, 68, 88
Benoist-Méchin, Baron Jacques, 145, 152
Bergeret, General, 146-7
Blomberg, Major Axel von, 105-6
Brauchitsch, Field-Marshal Walter von, 162
Brazzaville, 123
Brenner meeting, 60-1
Britain, 11, 13, 19, 21, 24: relations with France, 12; relations with Vichy France, 34; policy towards Palestine, 47; blockade of Syria by, 71, 74-5; rejects proposed partition of Syria, 152; tension between Britain and Free France, 157
Bulgaria, 61-2, 67, 69, 161

Cadogan, Sir Alexander, 138, 139, 160
Cairo, 27, 39-40, 45-6, 48, 61, 122, 123, 130, 132, 150
Cameroons, 40, 47
Canada, 171
Catroux, General Georges, 47-8, 64, 70-2, 76, 122-3, 127-35, 139-40, 153-5
Cavallero, General, 118
Churchill, Sir Winston, 21, 30, 47-8, 64, 68-9, 89-90, 93, 99,

Index

109-10, 112, 125, 129, 131, 135-6, 139, 150-1, 155, 158, 159-60, 166-70

Ciano, Count, 27, 37, 51, 53-4, 56, 97-8, 143

Constantinople, 60

Conty, M., 147-9, 151

Cornwallis, Sir Kinahan, 86, 88-94, 100

Crete, 62, 69, 89, 99, 113, 115, 123, 135-7, 139, 159, 164; German assault on, 134

Cripps, Sir Stafford, 161

Cyprus, 115, 123, 136, 137, 144, 165

Cyrenaica, 67, 136, 137

Dakar, 47-8

Darlan, Admiral Jean François, 103, 127, 129, 141-2, 145, 146, 151

Damascus, 12, 13, 18, 57, 73, 75, 78, 122, 130-1, 135, 136, 145, 147, 148n., 157; fall of, 147

De Gaulle, President Charles, 32, 47-8, 70, 73, 122-4, 127, 129-30, 132, 134, 140, 142, 149-50, 152-7

Dentz, General Henri, 70-7, 106, 124, 126-7, 130-1, 135, 140, 143-5, 147-8, 151-3, 155

Derna, 67, 88

Dill, Sir John, 85-6, 110, 124, 126, 136, 161, 169-70

Druze minorities, 13, 14, 70, 72, 140

Eden, Anthony, *later* Lord Avon, 76 85, 88, 93, 123, 130-1, 133, 137, 138-9, 149, 157, 161

Egypt, 1, 6, 21, 24-8, 34, 39, 49, 57, 60, 62, 69-70, 81-3, 97, 101, 109, 111, 119-20, 133, 141, 158, 159, 161-2, 164, 167-70; independence granted, 15

Engert, Cornelius van, 75, 77, 118, 121, 147-8, 151, 152

Epirus, 89

EXPORTER codename, 136, 138, 139

Faris al-Khuri, 155

Farouk, King, 27, 119

Faysal, 12-13, 18-19, 158; made king of Iraq, 12

Felmy, General, 113, 116, 162

France, 11, 19, 24, 31, 73, 74, 82, 122, 125, 127, 140, 146, 158; fall of, 21, 31, 40

Franco-Syrian Treaty, 1936, 75

Free French, 35, 47-8, 70-2, 76, 122, 124, 128-32, 134, 135, 139, 140, 142, 147, 149-50, 152-7

French Popular Front government, 14

Freyberg, Cyril Bernard, Baron, 137

Gabbrielli, Luigi, 36-7, 51, 53, 56, 78-9, 96, 98-9, 114, 116

Germany, 19, 21-2, 25, 33, 38, 42-3, 49, 56, 73, 79-80, 81, 96: attitude to Arab nationalism, 40; strategy of, 57; plans dropped for invasion of Britain by, 59; tension between Germany and Soviet Union, 111

Gibraltar, 41, 58

Giorgis, General de, 143

Glubb, Major John Bagot (Glubb Pasha), 72, 112, 156

'Golden Square' group, 35, 78-9, 85-6, 94, 108, 117

Goutton, Admiral, 144

Graziani, Marshal Rodolfo, 57

Greece, 61-3, 67-9, 75-6, 81, 102, 123, 126, 136, 159, 170: Italian invasion of, 61, 63; German invasion of, 69, 88-9; British evacuation from, 94

Grobba, Fritz, 49, 101, 105, 108, 116

Guarnaschelli, Giovanni, 51-3

Habbaniya, 14, 86, 89, 94, 100, 107, 109-11, 113; break-out of hostilities at, 100-1

HABFORCE, 109, 111-13, 149n.

Haddad, Uthman Kamal, 49-51, 56, 81, 99; proposals made by, 49-53, 55

Haifa, 23, 24, 112, 144-5

Halder, Generaloberst Franz, 62

Halifax, Edward Frederick Lindley Wood, 1st Earl of, 64-5

Hashim al-Atasi, 155

Hentig, Werner von, 72-5, 82, 106

Hess, Rudolf, flight of Hess to Scotland, 104

Hitler, Adolf, 17, 19, 37, 40-1,

Index

Index

Tobruk, 67, 68, 88
Transcaucasia, 161-2
Transjordan, 18, 29, 44, 50, 53, 72, 81, 96, 109
Transjordan Frontier Force, 112-13
Tripoli, 23, 136, 149n.
TROUT, contingency plan codename, 23, 36
Turkey, 11, 34, 37, 54, 59, 61-4, 68-71, 81-3, 92, 97, 100, 108, 110, 115, 118, 133, 137-8, 143, 161-3, 164, 167, 171; mediation proposed by, 107-8
Tunisia, 25

United States of America, 57, 65, 72, 75, 124, 162, 166, 171: entry of into World War II, 162-3; defence of Middle East rated as fourth priority by, 171-2

Vichy France, government of, 24, 31, 33-5, 45, 48, 59, 70, 72, 76, 103, 106, 122-8, 135, 138-9 142, 143-7, 150-3, 156, 167, 171

Wavell, General Archibald, 1st Earl, 22-3, 27, 33, 36, 45, 57, 64, 67-71, 75, 88-90, 106, 108-12, 118, 120, 121, 123-4, 128-32, 134-40, 149, 159, 168
Weizmann, Chaim, 29
Weizsäcker, Ernst von, 53, 55-6, 84
Welles, Sumner, 125
Weygand, General Maxime, 32, 70-2
Wilson of Libya, Field-Marshal Lord, 26, 112, 136, 140, 151
Woermann, Ernst, 81-4, 95-6, 104

Yemen, 111
Yugoslavia, 61: anti-German *coup* in, 69; German invasion of, 88-9

Zionist movement, 16-17

180